Bicycling the Uncompahgre Plateau

by **Bill Harris**

PRESS

Ouray, Colorado

Published by Wayfinder Press
Post Office Box 1877
Ouray, Colorado 81427

Manufactured in the United States of America

Typesetting - Text, The Typeshop
                    Maps, CJ Typesetting
Cartography - Keith Abernathy
Artwork - Mike Wittmer
Cover Design - Clarke Cohu
Photography - Bill Harris
Contributing Writer - Chapter 4, Gordon C. Tucker, Jr.
Copyediting - Rose Houk

ISBN 0-943727-11-1

To Ruth, Peter, Dolores and Bill

Acknowledgments

I would like to express my sincere gratitude to the many people who provided encouragement, support and suggestions. A special thanks to Mike Wittmer, Keith Abernathy and Gordy Tucker for their superb contributions. Technical assistance from Sharon Manhart, Linda Delman, Henry Kuntz, The Typeshop, CJ Typesetting and Doug and Jura Harris helped pull everything together. I would be remiss if I didn't thank all my trail companions, whose enthusiasm and friendship furnished an added incentive to keep cranking off the miles. Finally I must express my love and appreciation to my family, Kathy, Tony and Mindi.

Contents

Preface

The popularity of off-road bicycling has skyrocketed in recent years. Many trails and jeep roads are witnessing an ever-increasing number of biking enthusiasts as mountain bikers seek new ways to pedal into the backcountry. Many are discovering off-road biking havens close to their own backyards. This guidebook is about one such haven: The Uncompahgre Plateau of west-central Colorado.

The Uncompahgre Plateau eludes the usual standards used to describe the backcountry. Wildness prevails in spite of a maze of jeep roads that reaches into all but a few areas. One of the largest deer herds in Colorado and a substantial population of elk, bear and mountain lion bespeak the plateau's wildness. The plateau cannot boast of snow-capped peaks and pristine lakes, but the deep canyons, the fingerlike tablelands and distant vistas of surrounding mountain ranges compare favorably with any scenic area in the West.

From afar, the plateau's low profile gives the illusion of flatness. Nothing could be further from the truth. A closer look reveals a maze of canyons and mesas. This rugged terrain, created by at least a million years of erosion, surrounds the plateau's relatively flat highland crest. Hundreds of miles of jeep roads, plus the beauty, serenity and ruggedness of the Uncompahgre Plateau combine to make it an ideal fat-tire bicycling locale.

This book is more than just a trail guide. It describes the unique environment and history of the Uncompahgre Plateau and will be useful to any backcountry traveler who ventures there.

The first five chapters offer an overview of the

plateau's geography, resources, geology, natural history, prehistory and history. Chapter Six contains an access road map and describes the main access roads. Chapter Seven lists twenty bicycling trails. The trails are numbered and correspond with the trail numbers on the maps found in that chapter. Each trail description includes elevation, distance, rating, bicycling season, access, maps and highlights.

REGIONAL MAP
West-Central Colorado

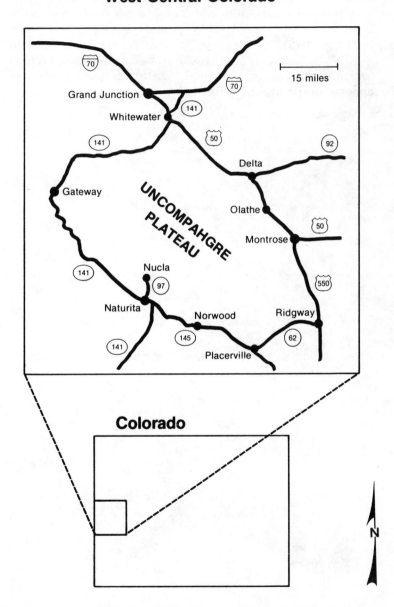

CHAPTER 1
THE PLATEAU

GEOGRAPHY

The Uncompahgre Plateau occupies a large part of west-central Colorado. It is 100 miles long, 25 to 30 miles wide, and is oriented in a southeast-northwest direction. It ranges from the San Juan Mountains to the Utah-Colorado border, west of Grand Junction, Colorado. The Uncompahgre Plateau is more accurately defined as an uplift, which developed its present stature about one million years ago. Erosion has played a major role in the shaping of the innumerable arroyos, gulches and canyons that give the plateau its rugged relief. Tons of sand and silt are washed away yearly, contributing a significant amount of mass to the murky waters of five major rivers. The plateau narrowly avoids watery isolation from surrounding landforms at its extreme southern boundary where it butts up against the Sneffels Range of the San Juan Mountains.

The Uncompahgre Plateau is a land of contrasts. The highland crest is rolling, cool and wet, whereas the surrounding lowlands are deeply cut, hot and dry. The western flank drops off the crest in an abrupt descent to a maze of mesas and canyons. The eastern flank is characterized by an alternating series of long fingerlike mesas and deep canyons. Several of these mesas form a ramplike feature that gradually merges with the Uncompahgre Valley. The relatively level crest parallels the plateau's axis, breached only by Unaweep Canyon, which effectively isolates the northern third of the plateau from the remainder of the uplift.

Although the plateau possesses no dramatic peaks, it has several obvious high points along the crest: Wolf Hill, elevation 9,247 feet; Uncompahgre Butte, elevation 9,732 feet; Monument Hill, elevation 9,561 feet; Spruce Mountain, elevation 9,731 feet; and Horsefly Peak, elevation 10,347 feet. By and large, the drainages that flow off the eastern flank are much longer than their counterparts on the western flank. Two exceptions are Horsefly and Tabeguache creeks. Because of its special geographic qualities, the plateau offers unique biking opportunities among its highlands and canyons.

BACKCOUNTRY TRAVEL

Although much of the Uncompahgre Plateau is accessible by vehicle, the wilderness ethic of walk (and bike) softly should prevail. Avoid rearranging the landscape, use existing trails and roads, keep a clean camp, and haul out all your trash and any you find—leave no evidence of your passing.

Keep food out of the reach of foraging animals. Be sure human waste is buried. Toilet paper should be burned. Avoid polluting any water source, and properly treat or filter all drinking water. A sure-fire way to ruin any outing is by contracting a parasite such as giardia from contaminated water.

WEATHER:

As a general rule the weather on the plateau is dictated by elevation. Precipitation is less at lower altitudes. In the areas adjacent to the river valleys annual precipitation averages 10 inches. In the high country above 8,000 feet annual precipitation can be in excess of 30 inches.

Temperatures also vary with altitude. In the river valleys daytime summer temperatures reach into the 80s and 90s. Nighttime temperatures can drop into the 50s. High country extremes vary from the 70s in the day to the 40s at night. Spring and fall are the best seasons to travel at lower elevations. Summer is the most comfortable time to bike in the higher areas.

By April, most of the trails below 7,000 feet are dry. Spring showers and cool periods interrupt sunny, warm stretches during April and May. Late May through June is usually dry. The lower altitudes on the plateau are hot from June through August. The higher elevations are free of snow by mid-June and are warming up. During

July and August the high country is warm and afternoon thundershowers are the norm. These thunderstorms can be quite severe at times. A general cooling trend occurs in September and October. It is not unusual for an early snowstorm to blow in by late September.

The most important factor concerning weather is preparation for an unexpected change. Check short- and long-range forecasts before "heading into the hills," and pay close attention to changing local weather conditions. Be sure rain gear and extra clothing are packed. A sudden downpour can turn a passable road into a muddy quagmire. If the going gets sticky, pull off the road, find available shelter and wait out the storm. Be sure to avoid ridgetops and tall trees during a lightning storm, and stay out of drainages during heavy rains. Flash floods are possible during July and August.

NAVIGATION:

Travel on the Uncompahgre Plateau offers the same problems encountered in other mountainous backcountry areas. A thorough working knowledge of map reading and use of a compass is essential. The low profile of the plateau and the similarity of terrain require frequent map checks. Getting lost is no fun and can be deadly.

Good maps are essential. Seven-and-a-half minute and county maps are available from local businesses and the U.S. Geological Survey. The U.S.G.S. county maps, which are referenced in the trail sections in this book, are handy to use and the most up-to-date. A travel map available from the U.S. Forest Service provides an overall view of the plateau, as well as access road information.

BACKCOUNTRY SURVIVAL:

Although a working knowledge of backcountry survival skills is indispensable, use of common sense and development of an open, positive attitude goes a long way when dealing with a survival situation.

Due to the backcountry nature of the plateau, adequate preparation is essential. A dependable, sturdy

"Please close all gates," Spring Creek Rim Road

vehicle such as a pickup truck or a four-wheel-drive vehicle is recommended. Be sure a shovel, axe, bucket, handi-jack, common tools, extra oil, extra gas, 20-foot tow rope and extra water are loaded into the vehicle before departing. Bicycle equipment should include a tool kit, extra spokes, spare tubes and tires, lubricant, and a tire pump.

Camping gear should be durable, well-made and functional. A three-season sleeping bag, tent, cookstove, cooking equipment, rain gear and proper footwear are requisites.

Many survival experts emphasize that survival is a state of mind. A positive attitude, determination, adaptability, good judgment and resourcefulness are key traits in a survival situation. Another key survival concept is improvisation. Use the resources at your disposal to provide the basics for survival, namely shelter, water and food. A tried and true survival technique is the STOP method described in Gene Fear's book, "Surviving the Unexpected Wilderness Experience":

S - Stop: sit down and assess the situation

T - Think: think about the situation, analyze the variables, the weather, terrain and resources

O - Observe: look at the present danger and possible future dangers

P - Plan: after analyzing the situation, develop a plan of action that will be the safest, taking into consideration the resources available

Be sure the ten survival essentials are packed with your gear:

1. knife
2. waterproof matches and a candle
3. whistle
4. signal mirror
5. extra food
6. map and compass
7. flashlight and extra batteries
8. water treatment equipment
9. rain gear
10. first aid kit — know how to use it!

NATURAL HAZARDS:

As with any backcountry environment, natural hazards are part of the overall picture. Some weather hazards have been discussed already. Other hazards associated with weather include the effects of heat and cold. Prevention of heat stroke and hypothermia is easier than treatment of either. Proper protection from the effects of the sun on the body can be easily prevented by using a sunscreen and drinking enough fluids.

Other hazards can be divided into three categories. The first is poisonous and noxious plants. Poison ivy and stinging nettle can be found along water courses. Avoid eating wild plants or mushrooms unless a positive identification has been made. Oakbrush thickets should be avoided due to their tenacious and frustrating qualities. The second category is critters. Most critters will leave you alone if given a wide berth. Always be on the lookout for a sour bear with cubs, rattlesnakes and scorpions. Other critters will seek you out. Mosquitos, ticks, deer flies, and the ubiquitous "no-see-ums" can be deterred with appropriate repellents. The third category is terrain. Be careful when riding around rocky areas, slopes or rimrock. Wear a safety helmet at all times.

ROAD AND TRAIL CONDITIONS:
Road and trail conditions can vary widely on the plateau. They can be rocky, sandy, graveled, smooth, hard-packed, muddy or any combination of the above. Weather and elevation have a direct influence on road and trail conditions.

Turn back when conditions warrant. Exercise extra caution with stream crossings during spring runoff or following heavy rains.

PRIVATE PROPERTY:
Although most of the Uncompahgre is public land, there are numerous private in-holdings. Mining claims, springs, grazing areas, cow camps and summer cabins make up the bulk of these holdings. Please honor locked gates and no trespassing signs, and refrain from damaging fences or buildings. The roads and trails in this book are open to public access. The Forest Service travel map has other access roads marked. During the summer, the plateau is grazed by sheep and cattle. Give livestock a wide berth if they are encountered on the roads or trails and do not harass them.

RESOURCES
There are no developed facilities or services on the plateau, but they are available in the surrounding towns. Grand Junction offers the largest selection of goods and services of interest to the backcountry traveler. It has a number of sporting goods stores with a variety of items in all price ranges. Several bike shops offer a full line of parts, and well-equipped service departments. A bike shop in Montrose can make most

Old Paradox Road

repairs, and has a limited selection of biking gear. Delta
and Montrose have sporting goods stores, with a limited
selection of gear. Grand Junction, Montrose, Delta,
Ridgway, Norwood, Nucla and Naturita have grocery
stores, but the smaller the town, the smaller the selection.
Gas and garage services are available in all these towns,
and gas is also available in Whitewater, Gateway and
Placerville. Restaurants and motels are located in most
of the communities surrounding the plateau. Topographic maps (7.5 minute and county) can be obtained
from the sporting goods stores in Grand Junction,
Montrose and Delta. Forest Service and Bureau of Land
Management (BLM) maps are available at offices listed
below.

Most of the Uncompahgre Plateau is managed by
either the U.S. Forest Service or the BLM. Both agencies

can provide up-to-date information concerning weather and road conditions.

The Dominguez, Antone Spring, Columbine, Iron Spring and Divide Fork campgrounds have sites available on a first-come, first-serve basis. They have toilet facilities, water and tables. The campgrounds are located along or near the Divide Road. Primitive camping is allowed elsewhere on the plateau. Ranger stations at Cold Springs, Columbine Pass and Silesca Pond are staffed on a limited basis during the summer. The Forest Service and BLM offices listed below are open Monday through Friday, excluding holidays.

Forest Service

2505 South Townsend
Montrose, Colorado 81401
(303) 249-3711

Supervisor's Office
225 Highway 50
Delta, Colorado 81416
(303) 874-7691

Forest Ranger's Office
1760 Grand Avenue
Norwood, Colorado 81423
(303) 327-4261

BLM

District Office

2465 South Townsend
Montrose, Colorado 81401
(303) 249-7791

Highway 141
East of Norwood, Colorado
(303) 327-4407

Atkinson Creek Road

CHAPTER 2
GEOLOGY

When one looks at the Uncompahgre Plateau, it is hard to imagine that it is part of the ancestral Rocky Mountains. The plateau, a remnant of the anticlinal uplift called Uncompahgria, had its origin 310 million years ago near the end of the Mississippian Period. The uplift was reactivated several times during late Jurassic and late Cretaceous times, before reaching its present stature in the late Cenozoic Era around a million years ago. The upward arching of the plateau's rock strata is quite obvious along its southwestern flank near Windy Point. Here the terrain precipitously drops more than 2,000 feet in a series of cliffs and slopes from the plateau's crest. This impressive bit of real estate offers the most strenuous bike trails on the plateau.

Erosion has stripped off thousands of feet of rock that once overlaid the present strata on the plateau, contributing a substantial amount of mass to many of the geologic formations of the Colorado Plateau. In several places along Dominguez, Escalante and Unaweep canyons, and also in the upper reaches of Blue and Mesa creeks, erosion has cut down to Precambrian rock, commonly called "basement rock." The Dakota Formation, which has resisted erosion, forms the caprock over much of the plateau.

Probably the most interesting aspect of Uncompahgre Plateau geology is Unaweep Canyon, located between Whitewater and Gateway. At one time, according to some geologists, the combined waters of the Gunnison and Colorado rivers flowed through Unaweep Canyon across the plateau's spine, and joined the Dolores River near the town of Gateway. During the last uplift, the ancestral waters were not able to cut into the Precambrian rock fast enough to keep pace with the uplift. The riverbed was abandoned, and the waters diverted around the northern flank of the plateau, creating the present-day Horsethief, Ruby and Westwater canyons of the Colorado River.

The 3,000-foot-deep Unaweep Canyon was also the scene of geologic activity during Pleistocene times. The canyon was filled with huge tongues of glacial ice, which molded and smoothed the canyon walls into the familiar U-shape of a glacial valley. Today two undersized streams, East Creek and West Creek, flow in opposite directions from the highest point of the canyon.

Other locales where the geologic history of the Uncompahgre Plateau is particularly well-exposed are the Dolores River and Dominguez, Escalante, Tabeguache and Roubideau creeks. The Chinle, Wingate, Navajo, Kayenta, Morrison and Dakota formations in these areas display an impressive assortment of relief, texture and color reminiscent of the canyon country of Utah.

The geologic formations of the plateau have provided economic opportunities for the local inhabitants. Copper, uranium, radium and vanadium have been extracted from the Morrison Formation. Granite, quarried from Unaweep Canyon, was used to build Colorado's state capitol.

Further information about Uncompahgre Plateau geology can be obtained from the Colorado Geologic Survey. It has assembled an excellent geologic map and self-guided tour titled "Scenic Trips into Colorado Geology: Uncompahgre Plateau." The publication explains the plateau's geology in terms easily understood by the layman and is available in stores that handle topographic maps.

Unaweep Canyon

CHAPTER 3
NATURAL HISTORY

PLANTS

    The plants of the Uncompahgre Plateau typify those found in the uplands of the Colorado Plateau. The diversity of plant life on the plateau, in large part, is due to elevation. An increase in elevation with a respective increase in coolness and wetness establishes different sets of environmental conditions which predetermine the types of plants that will survive. Soil type, exposure, drainage, wind and available sunlight are other variables which play a role in determining plant selectivity.

    Each plant has its own niche. Some species tolerate a range of conditions, others thrive in a very specific environment. For instance, the common dandelion can be found throughout the plateau, whereas Eastwood's monkeyflower is limited to an environment found in a few seep alcoves.

    The Uncompahgre Plateau hosts four general plant zones or belts with their respective species. The elevation at which these belts can be found is not uniform, due to a gradual transition from one zone to another and differences in topography and exposure. An example: pinyon pine and Utah juniper can be found in association with scrub oak and yellow pine on dry mesas and south-facing slopes at around 8,000 feet. Aspen and Douglas fir will intermingle with scrub oak and yellow pine on wetter, north-facing slopes at about the same elevation.

    The plant zone that dominates the landscape below 7,500 feet is the pinyon-juniper belt, also called the p-j woodland. Pinyon pine, Utah juniper, greasewood, rabbitbrush, mormon tea and several species of sagebrush are the dominant trees and shrubs of the woodland. Several varieties of grass, cactus and yucca, as well as Indian paintbrush, locoweed, scarlet gilia, desert phlox, evening primrose, sego lily and desert four-o'clock call the woodland home. Annual precipitation averages between 10 and 20 inches. Streamside plants in this belt include the narrowleaf cottonwood, scrub oak, willow, tamarisk, virgin's bower, poison ivy and box elder. Of special interest in the pinyon-juniper belt is a specialized community called cryptogamic soil. It is a combination of slow-growing algae, lichens and fungi that forms a black, superficial crust on sandy soil. It protects the soil from erosion and absorbs moisture. Walking, driving, or bicycling on this delicate crust will break down its soil-holding capacity.

At around 7,000 feet the oak-pine belt begins to replace the "p-j." Gambel oak (scrub oak) and ponderosa pine (yellow pine) are the dominant trees in this habitat. Serviceberry, mountain mahogany, Rocky Mountain juniper, Oregon grape, green manzanita and wild rose

Evening primrose

are the shrubby inhabitants of this belt. Aspen, black birch, black alder and chokecherry can be found along the streams. Pasque flower, lupine, blue flag, sulphur flower, cushion buckwheat, kinnikinnick, sticky aster and coyote mint are a few of the blooming plants found on the forest floor. Precipitation in the oak-pine belt ranges between 20 and 25 inches annually.

Between 8,000 and 8,500 feet the oak-pine belt gives way to the aspen-fir belt. Annual precipitation has now increased to 25 or 30 inches yearly. Aspen forests dominate the terrain. Douglas fir can be found scattered among the aspens and along water courses. Common juniper, thimbleberry and mountain lover are found growing on the forest floor. Spring beauty and fawn lily are some of the earliest blooming plants, followed by columbine, wild violet, wild strawberry, mariposa lily, American vetch, cinquefoil, harebell and several varieties of penstemon.

The spruce-fir belt is the wettest, coldest and highest environment found on the plateau. It begins around 9,500 feet, and annual precipitation averages between 30 and 50 inches. The growing season is quite short and offers the harshest growing conditions on the plateau. Englemann spruce (hanging cones) and subalpine fir (upright cones) are the key species of the zone. Thick stands of these conifers are occasionally broken by small meadows filled with shrubs and wildflowers. Blue spruce, wolf currant and willow are also inhabitants of this cool, moist environment. Blooming plants of the spruce-fir belt include marsh marigold, delphinium, columbine, monkshood, rosecrown, flax, Jacob's ladder, bluebells, orange paintbrush and parrot's beak.

For centuries man has harvested the bounty of the plateau. Prehistoric peoples used plants for food, shelter, medicine, tools and religious purposes. Since the 1880s livestock grazing and timber cutting have been the focus of activity. During the first two decades of grazing and logging, the health of the plateau's plant life was severely impacted. Since the early 1900s, conservation efforts of the federal government and concerned citizens have helped restore the health and beauty of the plateau's greenery.

ANIMALS

The Uncompahgre Plateau is home for a great variety of mammals, birds and several species of reptiles, fish and amphibians. Elk, mule deer, mountain lion, bobcat, coyote, fox and porcupine range throughout the plateau.

Cottontail rabbits, jackrabbits, badgers, packrats, chipmunks and rock squirrels, as well as lizards, toads and the faded pygmy rattlesnake inhabit the plateau's lower elevations. Small populations of desert bighorn sheep and pronghorn can be found in isolated areas at the plateau's northeast boundary.

Inhabitants of higher elevations include the vole, pocket gopher, golden-mantled squirrel, gray squirrel, marmot, snowshoe hare, pine marten and ermine. Black bears range above 8,000 feet, but are seldom seen due to their timid nature.

Beaver, muskrat, leopard frogs, salamanders and trout inhabit the plateau's streams and ponds.

The plateau's airspace is patrolled by bats, ravens, pinyon jays, canyon wrens, red flickers, downy woodpeckers, black-capped chickadees, lazuli buntings, juncos, loggerhead shrikes, magpies, Steller's jays, evening grosbeaks, mountain bluebirds, mourning doves, cliff swallows, hummingbirds, Clark's nutcrackers and kingfishers. Raptors include red-tailed hawk, Cooper's hawk, goshawk, great horned owl, flammulated owl, screech owl, golden eagle and bald eagle. Gambel's quail, sage grouse, pheasant, blue grouse and chukar are the primary game birds that inhabit the plateau. The wild turkey population was substantial at one time, but became diseased and was removed from the plateau. Plans call for the reintroduction of the species.

The wildlife of the plateau has always been a source of food for man. In prehistoric times, many species were hunted and trapped. Since the arrival of the white man,. the large game animals have garnered the hunter's attention. Unregulated hunting prior to the 1900s brought the herds of game animals to near extinction. The creation of a state game and fish commission reversed that trend. During the years before World War I, hunting was strictly regulated. After the war, Commissioner

Collared lizard

Roland Parvin and Game Warden Otto Peterson led the fight to preserve Colorado's wildlife. Peterson's reputation was legendary. He pursued and apprehended poachers with uncanny proficiency. His tough and unpredictable nature commanded respect from all who knew him. Today the Colorado Division of Wildlife manages the game and nongame species of the Uncompahgre country.

CHAPTER 4
PREHISTORY

The prehistory of the Uncompahgre Plateau has attracted considerable attention since the 1920s. W. C. McKern, Harold Huscher, C. T. Hurst, Marie Wormington, Robert Lister, William Buckles and David Breternitz, to name just a few, have investigated archaeological sites on or near the Uncompahgre Plateau. As a result of the efforts of these individuals, we now know that people have lived on the Uncompahgre Plateau for at least 10,000 years. This long period of occupation is divided into four major cultural stages, each stage defined by a particular way of life. The stages are briefly described below.

PALEOINDIAN STAGE (CA. 10,000-5500 B.C.)
Evidence that Paleoindian peoples occupied west-central Colorado is extremely sparse. This evidence so far is limited to surface finds of distinctive projectile point types. From localities where Paleoindian remains are more abundant (such as southern Wyoming and eastern Colorado), researchers have deduced that the focus of Paleoindian economic activity was the hunting of large game animals, many of which are now extinct. Paleoindian bands were highly mobile, moving through an annual territory in pursuit of large game. Temporary shelters probably were built, and various plant resources were undoubtedly exploited, but no direct evidence of such practices has yet been found.

Three traditions have been identified for the Paleoindian Stage, each characterized by distinctive projectile points found in association with particular animal species. The Llano Tradition (10,000-9000 B.C.) is characterized by the fluted Clovis point, found with the remains of extinct mammoth; the Folsom Tradition (9000-7000 B.C.) is distinguished by the fluted Folsom point, found in association with extinct forms of bison; and the Plano Tradition (7000-5500 B.C.) is distinguished by several types of unfluted projectile points (e.g., Agate Basin, Eden, Midland, Plainview and Scottsbluff), found in association with modern animals, such as pronghorn and bison. Folsom points and several types of points associated with the Plano Tradition have been found on the plateau.

ARCHAIC STAGE (5500 B.C.-A.D. 1)

The Archaic stage represents a shift away from a reliance upon large game towards a more diversified economy that was more equally divided between plants and animals. The Archaic Stage in west-central Colorado is extraordinarily persistent, overlapping with the Paleo-indian Stage and flourishing until European contact in historic times. Its longevity is perceived as a successful adaptation to a unique natural environment.

Archaic groups were highly mobile bands, moving throughout the year from one area to another as seasonal food resources became available. They probably set up base camps near these resources, staying there for up to several weeks, and established short-term campsites near the exploitable resources. The base camps were moved as these resources were depleted.

The annual subsistence of Archaic groups in west-central Colorado was oriented along drainage systems. Bands wintered along lower elevation valleys in the pinyon-juniper belt, moving into the higher elevations during the spring as the large game animals moved upslope and desirable plant resources became available; they returned to the lowland valleys as winter approached.

The best evidence for Archaic cultures on the Uncompahgre Plateau, like the rest of Colorado, comes from rockshelters. These are desirable habitations since they provide protection from the elements and are warm in winter (if they face south) and cool in summer. The debris left behind by the inhabitants is well-protected, and provides a detailed record of the regional culture history. Local examples of such sites include the Taylor,

Alva, Christmas, Moore and Casebier shelters, Tabeguache Caves, and the Harris Site.

Artifacts commonly found on Archaic sites in the region include mostly chipped stone (projectile points, knives, scrapers, drills and debris) and groundstone (manos and grinding slabs). Bone, antler and perishable items occasionally have been recovered from rockshelters. Archaic Stage sites in west-central Colorado are most often identified by the occurrence of distinctive projectile point types. These include large corner-notched points, large side-notched points, stemmed-indented base points, large side-notched indented base points, contracting stemmed points and stemmed square-base points. These implements were probably attached to an atlatl-propelled dart. Small corner-notched points, which may have been attached to arrows, appear near the end of the Archaic Stage.

Another aspect of prehistoric life commonly associated with the Archaic Stage is rock art. Rock art sites are common in this area. Most of the art is pecked or incised on rock surfaces (petroglyphs). Common elements include animal figures, abstract designs, animal footprints and human figures. Some of the rock art reflects influences from the Anasazi and Fremont cultures.

FORMATIVE STAGE (A.D. 1–1300)

West-central Colorado lies outside, or on the periphery, of two major Formative Stage cultures: the Anasazi Tradition, located in southwestern Colorado and Utah, Arizona and New Mexico; and the Fremont Tradition, located in Utah and northwestern Colorado. These groups farmed, typically growing corn, beans and squash, supplemented by wild foods; made pottery; and lived in permanent or semipermanent habitations made of stone or jacal (mud and sticks), or dug into the ground (pithouses).

Sites with possible Anasazi or Fremont cultural affiliations are sparse in the area, and generally are located in western Montrose County and in Mesa County near Grand Junction—that is, in those areas on the edge

The beautiful, but deadly, amanita muscaria

of the Anasazi and Fremont territories. The Formative Stage is recognized by the presence of cultivated foods, masonry habitation structures, and ceramics.

Remains of cultivated plants, mostly corn but some squash, have been found at about two dozen sites in the region, including Christmas Rockshelter, along Roubideau Creek, and in Tabeguache Caves I and II.

Structural remains are slightly more abundant than remains of cultivated plants, but the ranges of the two attributes overlap. The structures are primarily of two forms: rectangular and circular. The rectangular types are mostly found on the western slopes of the Uncompahgre Plateau and are probably Anasazi. The round structures are less common, found mostly on the eastern side of the plateau along the lower Gunnison River. They may be of Fremont origins.

About 600 Formative Stage ceramic fragments have so far been found in the region. Approximately 85 percent of these are Anasazi, the remainder are Fremont types.

Given the scarcity of these so-called culturally diagnostic attributes on sites in the region, and the fact that some of these "traits" have dubious validity, it is not surprising that many have questioned the idea that Fremont or Anasazi groups actually lived in the area. In fact, some researchers have speculated that indigenous Archaic people may have adopted a Formative Stage lifestyle. They exchanged ceramics with their Anasazi and Fremont neighbors, and adopted some of their architecture.

PROTO-HISTORIC STAGE (A.D. 1300–1881)

The Formative Stage lifeway, locally developed or not, apparently disappeared in the region about A.D. 1300, to be replaced by an Archaic-like lifestyle. This stage persisted in the region until the arrival of Euroamerican peoples in the late nineteenth century. It is commonly assumed that the area was occupied during most, if not all, of this period by Utes. Linguistic data have been used to estimate that ancestral Utes reached west-central Colorado between A.D. 1200 and 1400. However, firm evidence of Ute occupation in the region dates back to the eighteenth century.

Like their Archaic predecessors (or ancestors), the Ute pursued a nomadic, hunting and gathering lifestyle. Small bands moved through an annual territory exploiting seasonally available resources. Their artifacts were similar to Archaic except that they relied on the bow and arrow rather than atlatl and dart, and manufactured a distinct variety of pottery known as Uncompahgre Brown Ware. Euroamerican influence is evident on later Ute sites by the presence of glass buttons, glass beads, metal projectile points and metal ornaments. Adoption of the horse by the Utes increased their mobility and subtly altered their social structure. Rock art depicting horses or horselike figures, tipis and other historic elements are quite common in the region.

Ute sites are difficult to identify because their artifacts resemble those of earlier cultures. Those that have been identified as Ute contain wickiups, Uncompahgre Brown Ware sherds, Euroamerican trade items, or are associated with historic aboriginal rock art.

ARCHAEOLOGICAL ETHICS

Archaeological sites on the Uncompahgre Plateau are common. Those located on our public land are protected by federal and state laws. The removal of artifacts by surface collecting or digging effectively reduces the scientific potential of any site. Defacement of rock art has the same effect. Please help conserve cultural resources by leaving artifacts where they are found. Photographing artifacts and rock art is an alternative to collecting. If cultural resources are found on public land, please notify the managing federal agency.

By Gordon C. Tucker, Jr.

Archaic style rock art

CHAPTER 5
HISTORY

The history of the Uncompahgre country mirrors that of the American Southwest. The first Europeans to explore western Colorado were the Spanish. In 1776 Fathers Silvestre Velez de Escalante and Francisco Atanasio Dominguez led an expedition from Santa Fe, New Mexico, through western Colorado in search of a safe route to the missions of California. The priests, led by a Ute guide, traveled across the Uncompahgre Plateau, but never reached California.

By the early 1800s, intrepid mountain men began to filter into western Colorado in search of beaver. In 1828, Antoine Robidoux, a fur trapper, built Fort Uncompahgre near Delta, Colorado, which served as a supply station for trappers.

By 1850, the United States government had laid claim to territory which included western Colorado. The government's first order of business was to explore the new lands and evaluate their potential. In 1853, Captain John Gunnison led one of four engineering survey parties authorized by Congress to find a route for the railroad between the Mississippi Valley and the West Coast. Gunnison traveled across the Great Plains, through the San Luis Valley, over Cochetopa Pass and down the Gunnison River into the Uncompahgre Valley. Gunnison's expedition traveled as far west as the Sevier River in central Utah. There his party was attacked by hostile Paiutes and he was fatally wounded. The information he gathered depicted western Colorado as rugged and inhospitable, but it laid the groundwork for further exploration. Twenty years later, the Wheeler and Hayden surveys mapped much of the Uncompahgre country.

Between 1860 and 1880, western Colorado experienced a dramatic cultural transition. Prior to 1860, encroachment on Ute lands by whites had been minimal.

After the discovery of gold near Denver in 1858, and other areas of Colorado in the 1860s, Ute lands were inundated with prospectors and settlers. Conflict between the Utes and the trespassers resulted.

To avoid such conflicts, the Utes and the U.S. government negotiated a series of treaties between 1846 and 1879. With each treaty, the Utes ceded more of their lands. The Indians' primary spokesperson was Chief Ouray, a Tabeguache Ute. Ouray recognized the superiority of the government's political and military power, and hoped that a friendly posture towards the whites could be parlayed into a smaller but secure Ute homeland. Many of his fellow Utes did not see things as Ouray did. They resisted the takeover of their lands and attempts to convert them to a life of farming. The government set up several agencies to carry out the terms of the treaties, one of which was built near present-day Colona, Colorado. During the 1870s, treaty misunderstandings and unfulfilled promises led to an escalation in armed conflict.

By 1879, friction between the Utes and the whites had reached a feverish pitch. At the White River Agency in northwest Colorado, agent Nathan Meeker insisted on plowing the Utes' racetrack. This upset the Utes and an argument ensued. Meeker sent for military backup. The Utes interpreted this as an act of war and attacked the approaching military column, killing its commander, Major T. T. Thornburg. A few hours later, the Utes, led by Chief Douglas, attacked the agency. Meeker and the agency men were killed, and the women and children were taken hostage. These incidents, referred to as the Battle of Milk Creek and the Meeker Massacre, spawned a public outcry to place the remaining Utes on reservations. In September 1881 the White River and Uncompahgre Utes were assembled in the Uncompahgre Valley, then escorted to a reservation in northeast Utah.

The story of the Utes in Colorado cannot be told without mentioning gold and silver mining in the state. The mining districts of Crested Butte, Lake City, Creede, Ouray, Telluride and Silverton were located in the heart of Ute territory. The government was powerless to prevent miners from traveling into the rugged mountains in search of fortune. The general attitude among the fortune-seekers and most political leaders of the day was one of personal ambition and "manifest destiny." The whites argued that they could develop the Indian lands to their fullest potential. The removal of the Utes from northwestern and western Colorado opened the territory for settlement.

The frontier environment of the Uncompahgre country was one of excitement and growth. Emigrants quickly homesteaded available lands in the valleys surrounding the Uncompahgre Plateau. Miners flocked to the mining districts in the nearby mountains. Huge herds of cattle were grazed on summer range on the plateau, and timber was cut to provide lumber for mines and buildings. An economy based on the development of natural resources flourished.

Hanging flume along the Dolores River

Weathered stock corral

Most of the modern-day towns in the surrounding valleys were founded in the 1880s. These towns became the economic, social and political lifeblood of the Uncompahgre country.

In 1882 the Denver and Rio Grande Railroad extended its tracks into the Uncompahgre Valley by way of Marshall Pass. Otto Mears, dubbed "Pathfinder of the San Juans," was responsible for construction of the first roads in west-central Colorado and the Rio Grande Southern Railroad. By 1891 rails connected all the major mining areas of southwestern Colorado. Another enterprising Coloradan, Dave Wood, built a freight road between Montrose and Telluride in 1882.

In the 1880s, the cattle industry quickly developed on the Uncompahgre Plateau. Tens of thousands of cattle were moved to summer range on the plateau. In the fall, the animals were herded to rail stations in Montrose, Placerville and Whitewater, then shipped to eastern population centers. Competition for grazing lands was fierce. The rule of "first use" loosely regulated grazing rights, resulting in a range so heavily grazed that, by the early 1900s, the ground was barren in many areas of the plateau.

Around the turn of the century, two developments greatly influenced the ranching community. The first was the establishment of federal land reserves to regulate the use of resources on those lands, with conservation a prime goal. Grazing permits and quota systems were granted to those wishing to use the reserved lands. These reserves are known today as national forests, regulated by the U.S. Forest Service in the Department of Agriculture. Enactment of the Taylor Grazing Act of 1934 and creation of the Bureau of Land Management in 1946 created additional restrictions on the use of public domain.

The second development to influence the cattle industry on the Uncompahgre Plateau was introduction of sheep to the range. Cattlemen were bitterly opposed, and violence against the sheepmen was common. Delta County was a stronghold of sheep resistance. After 1920 tension between cowboy and sheepherder gradually eased. Today, as in past decades, cattle and sheep are grazed on the plateau. Weathered corrals and fence lines, cow camps and aspen tree art serve as faint reminders of earlier days of livestock operations.

With the settlement of west-central Colorado came the demand for lumber. The Uncompahgre Plateau supported as many as a dozen lumber mills at the turn of the century. The lumber industry harvested the large stands of aspen, spruce and ponderosa pine. It, too, came under government control with the establishment of forest reserves. Timber in the Uncompahgre National Forest now is managed by the Forest Service.

While mining, cattle and logging industries concentrated their activities in the nearby highlands, agriculturists were experimenting with a variety of crops in the valleys adjacent to the plateau. Staple crops such as potatoes, beans, onions, wheat, fruit and sugar beets were grown successfully. Feed crops included alfalfa and corn. Initially, scarcity of water limited crop production, but irrigation systems were developed to water arable lands. Waters from the Uncompahgre, Gunnison and San Miguel rivers as well as many feeder streams were diverted for agricultural use. Agriculture remains the economic backbone of Uncompahgre country, despite financial hard times. Crop diversification, more efficient farming methods and aggressive marketing may help turn the tide.

Although the successful mining of precious metals was limited to nearby mountains, the discovery of carnotite ore in western Montrose County in 1891 led to a boom/bust mining industry. Carnotite ore contains radium, vanadium and uranium. With the development of uses for these rare elements, demand increased. Radium was used for scientific and medical purposes. Vanadium was extracted from the ore for use as a strengthening alloy in steel and iron between World War I and World War II. Before World War II, uranium had limited known uses, but development of the atomic bomb and nuclear power changed that.

The discovery of radium, vanadium and uranium in other parts of the world, plus a worldwide decrease in the demand for the elements, have virtually shut down carnotite ore mining in the west end of the Uncompahgre country. The canyon country along the lower Dolores and San Miguel rivers is littered with reminders of the uranium boom days. Recent activity has centered mainly on massive efforts to clean up and isolate the radioactive byproducts of past milling operations.

Since before the 1900s the involvement of the federal government has had a major impact in the development of the economic factors in west-central Colorado. The regulatory nature of the government's land use policies, while not always popular, has provided the needed mangement of natural resources on public land.

Preservation of the Uncompahgre Plateau's unique environment depends on careful mangagement of its resources. If proper management is maintained, the plateau can serve this generation while being protected for the use and enjoyment of future generations.

Aspen tree art

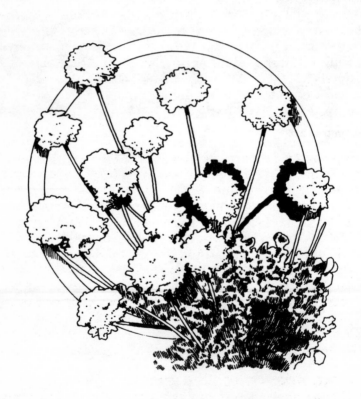

CHAPTER 6
ACCESS

HIGHWAYS

With one exception, paved roads skirt the perimeter of the Uncompahgre Plateau. The one exception, Highway 141, short-cuts the perimeter and travels along the line of least resistance, Unaweep Canyon. Five miles south of Grand Junction, Highway 141 branches from Highway 50 and 550 near Whitewater. It climbs 9 Mile Hill before winding along the floor of Unaweep Canyon. Forty-four miles from Whitewater, the road passes through Gateway along the banks of the Dolores River. Highway 141 then continues up the spectacular canyons of the Dolores and San Miguel rivers before turning south, four miles east of Naturita. Highway 97 is a short spur connecting the towns of Nucla and Naturita.

As Highway 141 turns away from the plateau, Highway 145 picks up and heads east over Wrights Mesa to the town of Norwood. A few miles east of Norwood, Highway 145 drops into the beautiful San Miguel River canyon, then snakes upriver where it intersects Highway 62 near Placerville. Highway 145 continues on to Telluride, while Highway 62 climbs over Dallas Divide, passes north of the Sneffels Range, then drops into the town of Ridgway. At Ridgway, Highway 62 intersects with Highway 550 which proceeds north along the Uncompahgre River, and down the Uncompahgre Valley to Montrose. In Montrose, Highway 550 merges with Highway 50, and they turn northwest, passing through Olathe and Delta before reaching Whitewater.

BACKCOUNTRY ACCESS ROADS

The Uncompahgre Plateau is linked by a network of improved, seasonally maintained back roads, strategically located to allow access to most of the plateau's real estate. The roads have played an important part in the

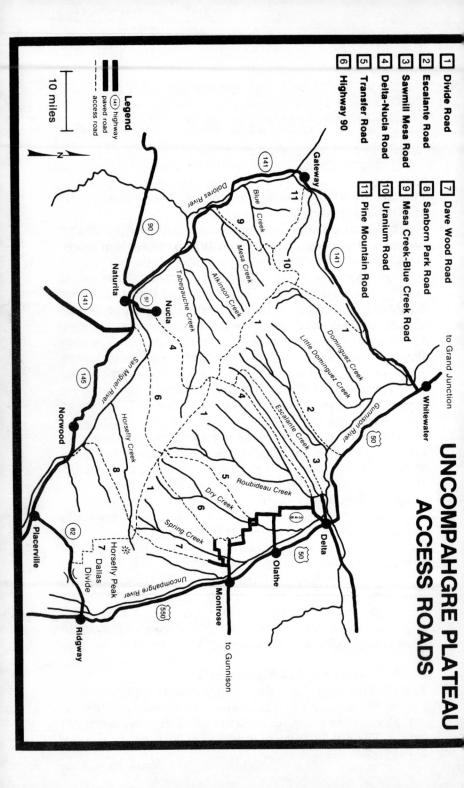

UNCOMPAHGRE PLATEAU
ACCESS ROADS

1. Divide Road
2. Escalante Road
3. Sawmill Mesa Road
4. Delta-Nucla Road
5. Transfer Road
6. Highway 90
7. Dave Wood Road
8. Sanborn Park Road
9. Mesa Creek-Blue Creek Road
10. Uranium Road
11. Pine Mountain Road

Legend
(141) highway
— — paved road
– – – – access road

10 miles

N

history of the plateau and have provided a vital link between the rugged backcountry and the amenities of surrounding communities.

DIVIDE ROAD:
By far the longest access road is the Divide Road. It begins in Unaweep Canyon, 15 miles from Whitewater. The Divide Road climbs to the crest of the plateau and parallels it until it reaches the Dave Wood Road, 82 miles from Unaweep Canyon. The scenery and distant vistas between Unaweep Canyon and Windy Point are spectacular. The anticlinal nature of the plateau can best be viewed from the Divide Road in the vicinity of Monument Hill and Windy Point. Between Windy Point and the road's southern terminus, it winds through dense stands of aspen, fir and spruce, virtually blocking any overlook possibilities. One exception is an overlook of Tabeguache Basin near Columbine Pass. Many of the cow camps used by ranchers since the late 1880s are adjacent to the Divide Road. The Divide Road intersects five other access roads on the plateau, easily making it the plateau's most important road. The plateau's display of fall colors are best viewed from the Divide Road.

DIVIDE ROAD MILEAGE LOG

Mile	Description
0	Road begins in Unaweep Canyon
1.8	Granite quarry
6.1	Turnoff to Dominguez Recreation Site
10.0	Carson Hole (picnic ground)
15.8	Uranium Road
15.9	Divide Fork Campground
20.0	Cold Springs Ranger Station turnoff
22.2	Dominguez and Brushy Ridge trails access
25.5	California Springs (campsite)

26.8	Uncompahgre Butte
28.5	Campbell Point Road
33.5	Turnoff to The Tongue
36.7	Love Mesa Road
37.6	T-Bone Springs (campsite)
39.2	Windy Point - 47 Trail
49.6	Delta-Nucla Road merges with Divide Road (33 miles to Delta)
49.7	Columbine Ranger Station
49.8	Columbine Campground
50.5	Columbine Pass, Delta-Nucla Road branches off (21 miles to Nucla)
51.0	Scenic Turnoff - views of Tabeguache Basin
54.9	7N Mesa Road
62.3	Hauser Road
65.5	Transfer Road and Antone Spring Campground (27 miles to Olathe)
66.7	South Highway 90 (27 miles to Highway 141)
66.9	Iron Spring Campground
67.7	North Highway 90 (23 miles to Montrose)
73.5	Beaver Dams Road
82.4	Spring Creek Rim Road
82.7	Divide Road intersects with Dave Wood Road

ESCALANTE ROAD:

The Escalante Road begins 12 miles northwest of Delta off Highway 50. The graveled road winds down to the Gunnison River, crosses it, then enters Escalante Canyon. As the road follows the meanders of the canyon, the walls rise up in an impressive display of canyon country hues. Three miles from the Gunnison River, the Dry Fork merges with the main canyon. Ranch houses, orchards and fields fill the canyon floor for the first 11 miles.

Escalante Canyon was settled soon after the Utes were relocated. Its protected, well-watered environment provided a suitable setting for homesteading. The Musser family, one of the first to move into the area, still operates the 6-D Ranch from its headquarters at the mouth of the canyon. A few miles past the Dry Fork confluence are the remains of a stone house built in 1911 by Harry Walker. Table Rock, a flat-topped rock pillar, is farther up the canyon. Ben Lowe, a colorful early-day resident, resided in the ranch house near the base of Table Rock.

Divide Road vista

Another well-known canyon resident, Captain Henry Smith, built the cabin a mile farther up the canyon, using a large sandstone boulder for one of the cabin walls. Capt. Smith was a tombstone carver, and used his talents to carve his name on the boulder and a shelf inside the cabin which served as a bed. On the canyon wall above the cabin a horseshoe and a star are carved in the rock along with many historic signatures.

SAWMILL MESA ROAD:

The Sawmill Mesa Road parallels the Delta-Nucla Road to the east. Sawmill Mesa was originally called Briggs Mesa in honor of one of the Roberts Brothers' stud horses, but was renamed when one of the plateau's first sawmills was set up on the mesa. The Sawmill Mesa Road can be reached by driving west on Fifth Street in Delta. The street becomes a country lane that soon crosses Roubideau Creek. After climbing out of the drainage, the road travels along a bench west of Sawmill Mesa. As the road reaches the highlands, it intersects the Cottonwood Road which connects Love Mesa and 25 Mesa.

DELTA-NUCLA ROAD:

The Delta-Nucla Road connects the towns of Delta and Nucla. From Nucla it switchbacks around Big Bucktail Creek and across Tabeguache Basin before topping out at Columbine Pass. Tabeguache Basin is one of the wildest locales on the plateau—rugged, beautiful terrain steeped in history and legend. Back in the early 1880s a band of Utes intercepted a pair of Ouray sooners, who were checking out the basin for grazing potential. The Utes bullied the fellows into getting down on all fours to sample the grass for themselves. Stories of a lost gold mine and buried treasure also surface with regularity.

The northern section of the Delta-Nucla Road follows the gradual grade of 25 Mesa. Twenty-five Mesa was originally named Home Mesa by the Roberts Brothers, but the name did not stick. Its current name was coined when the area was mapped, and it was noted that the Roberts' summer camp was on Section

25. The ramplike character of the mesa did not go unnoticed by the plateau's prehistoric inhabitants. The mesa was part of a major trail between the San Miguel and Gunnison drainages. As the road comes off the plateau, it crosses Roubideau Creek, then bears to the east where it merges with Highway 348 a few miles southwest of Delta.

HIGHWAY 348:

Highway 348 is a paved state road. It zigzags across the lower Uncompahgre Valley and connects the towns of Olathe and Delta. Initially, Highway 348 travels west from Olathe. At Hoovers Corner the road turns north, then turns west again in a mile. The highway turns north once more at 5300 Road, and continues for 5.5 miles before the Delta-Nucla Road is encountered. Highway 348 then bears east and north as it heads into Delta. In Delta, Highway 348 can be reached by way of Eaton, 8th and Bridge streets.

TRANSFER ROAD:

The Transfer Road tracks up the eastern flank of the plateau between Roubideau and Dry creeks. The road is rough, but offers good access to several trails. The name "transfer" refers to the early-day practice of hauling milled lumber by sled from the Darling sawmill near the plateau's crest to a lower elevation where it was transferred to horse-drawn wagons. In the late 1890s and early 1900s, activity along the road was intense. Besides the sawmill operation, numerous families homesteaded quarter sections in hopes of making a life for themselves. An irrigation ditch was started to divert water from Roubideau Creek to Cushman Mesa. The ditch was never completed, and many of the homesteaders gave up due to harsh winters and isolation. Access to the Transfer Road from the Uncompahgre Valley is by way of Highway 348. Drive 5.5 miles west of Olathe, turn south on 5500 Road, then one mile east on Hickory Road.

HIGHWAY 90:

The uninitiated will be surprised by Highway 90's

Sneffels Range in the San Juan Mountains, from Highway 90

lack of pavement. The highway begins as a paved road in Montrose. It zigzags across Spring Creek Mesa, then drops into Shavano Valley. The road turns to gravel as it climbs out of the valley. Highway 90 crosses Dry Creek, then contours around several large hills that are filled with mule deer and wildflowers during the summer. The plant life along Highway 90 typifies the vegetation found on the Uncompahgre Plateau. The pinyon-juniper, oak-pine, aspen-fir and spruce-fir belts are well represented along the road. Soon after reaching the aspen-fir belt, the road passes by the Silesca Ranger Station. Highway 90 merges with the Divide Road two miles west of the ranger station. The highway barely gets settled into its new course when it drops off the crest of the plateau. The road contours around Red Canyon, traverses Tumble and Sheep creeks, then slips along Cottonwood Creek before it reaches the San Miguel River. Approximately 10 miles from the Divide Road, several buildings in various degrees of disrepair can be seen on both sides of the road. The dilapidated structures are what is left of Ute, a once-thriving rural community. Once across the San Miguel River, Highway 90 continues for another eight miles before reaching Highway 141, three miles east of Naturita.

DAVE WOOD ROAD:

The Dave Wood Road provides access to the southern end of the plateau. It begins on Spring Creek Mesa, west of Montrose. Turn south off of Highway 90 onto 62.50 Road. Dave Wood begins as the road turns to gravel. The road parallels Spring Creek to the west. In nine miles the road enters Forest Service land and winds through aspen groves. Some 21 miles from Montrose, the road converges on the southern terminus of the Divide Road. It immediately descends toward the broad valley of Horsefly Creek. One and one-half miles from the Divide Road, the Dave Wood Road meets the Sanborn Park Road (right fork). The left fork follows the modern-day equivalent of the road across Horsefly Mesa. Views of the Sneffels Range, and Wilson and Dolores peaks are possible from this vantage point. The road finally drops into Buck Canyon to meet Highway 62, four miles west of Dallas Divide.

The Dave Wood Road carries the name of the man who originally built it to haul freight between Montrose and Telluride in the 1880s. Completion of the Rio Grande Southern Railroad between Ridgway and Telluride in 1891 made the route obsolete.

SANBORN PARK ROAD:

The Sanborn Park Road begins at the bottom of Norwood Hill off of Highway 145. It follows the north bank of the San Miguel River for several miles, crosses Clay Creek, then abruptly switchbacks up to the canyon rim. The road soon mellows out and weaves through open meadows as well as thick stands of ponderosa pine and scrub oak. Cattle can be seen grazing in the meadows, and deer can be spotted along the forest's edge. The scenery is exceptional; views of the plateau's crest and distant peaks are possible. In June, wildflowers can be seen blooming everywhere.

Seventeen miles from the highway, the road crosses Horsefly Creek then continues for another three miles before meeting the Dave Wood Road. In the early days, Sanborn Park was a bustling community complete with a sawmill and a school.

URANIUM ROAD:

The Uranium Road begins at Divide Fork. It bears west, then south, before dropping off the west rim of the plateau. The road descends steadily to intersect with the Mesa Creek-Blue Creek Road and the Pine Mountain Road. As the name suggests, the Uranium Road was used to haul uranium from the many mines in the surrounding canyons. The uranium was hauled to a mill near Grand Junction as early as World War I. In more recent times, the ore was trucked over the Pine Mountain Road to Unaweep Canyon.

The road follows an old Indian trail that connected areas of winter and summer use. The terrain made accessible by the road is a wonderful maze of mesas and canyons that served its prehistoric inhabitants

Utah juniper

well, as evidenced by the high density of archaeological sites found in the area.

MESA CREEK-BLUE CREEK ROAD:

This access road connects Highway 141 and the
Uranium Road. It branches from Highway 141 26 miles
down-canyon from Naturita. The road, marked RD
P12, begins 0.2 mile down-canyon from the Mesa Creek
bridge, and heads north along Mesa Creek. After three
miles, the road forks. RD P12 continues to the right, the
Mesa Creek Road branches to the left and is marked
RD O14. At mile 11 the road climbs out of Mesa Creek
canyon, tops out, then descends quickly to Blue Creek.
At mile 15.5 the road again forks. The left fork con-
tinues to the Blue Creek Ranch. The right fork crosses
Blue Creek, then contours north where it intersects the

Uranium Road and the Pine Mountain Road at mile 21.5. Many side roads branch off the Mesa Creek-Blue Creek Road. Keep a map handy for quick reference. These roads lead to the many uranium prospects and mines that dot the surrounding landscape.

Campbell Point Road

CHAPTER 7
TRAILS

The trails described in this guide are a representative sampling of the biking possibilities on the Uncompahgre Plateau east and south of Unaweep Canyon, and all are on public land. Locked gates or posted lands may be encountered if the rider ventures onto trails not mentioned in this book. Questions concerning access, road construction and logging operations should be taken to the Forest Service or the BLM.

The trails highlighted in this guide travel through a wide variety of terrain. Each trail has its own personality and set of challenges. Some are easy, some are difficult.

Most of the trails below 7,000 feet are open through October, but big-game hunting seasons begin in early October. The plateau is filled with orange-clad hunters trying to fill their tags. The sound of regular gunfire and the lack of solitude deter most riders. If you do hit the trails during hunting season, wear a blaze-orange hat and jacket.

The scope of this guide is to provide the rider with the basic information needed to have a safe and enjoyable trip. Detailed information about the roads and trails is intentionally omitted to encourage careful planning and a sense of adventure. A selected bibliography is listed at the end of the guide for those who want to dig deeper. Most of the books can be found in local bookstores and libraries.

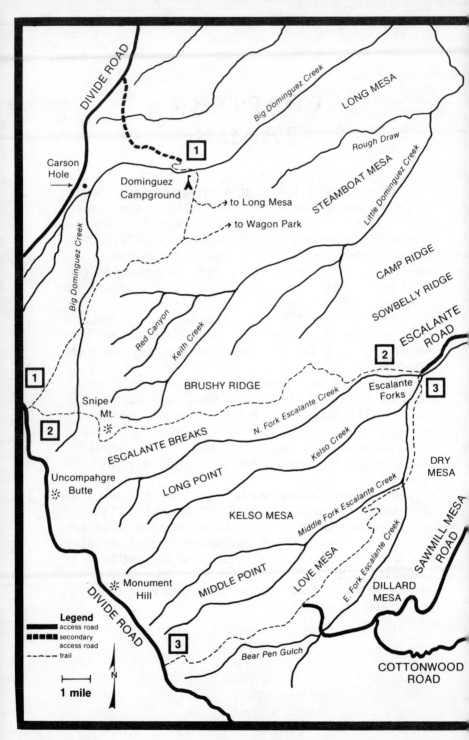

Trail Map One

1. DOMINGUEZ TRAIL

Elevation:	7,200–8,950 feet
Distance:	14 miles (one way)
Rating:	Moderate with two short steep sections
Season:	Mid-June to September
Access:	The Dominguez Trail can be reached from the Divide Road at two points. Six miles from Highway 141, the road to Dominguez Recreation Site branches from the Divide Road. Drive four miles on this road to the west rim of Dominguez Canyon. The upper end of the trail meets the Divide Road 6.3 miles south of the Divide Fork Campground.
Maps:	Trail Map One and U.S.G.S. Mesa County maps #5 & 6
Description:	The Dominguez Trail starts with a dramatic crossing of Dominguez Canyon. Once the canyon is negotiated, the trail settles down to a steady climb to the ridge dividing the Big and Little Dominguez drainages. From this high point, the trail descends to cross Dominguez Creek several miles upstream from the initial ford. Again the trail grades upward, then levels off before reaching the Divide Road.
Highlights:	Dominguez Creek was named by the 1874 Hayden Survey to honor one of the leaders of the 1776 Escalante-Dominguez

Expedition through western Colorado. Dominguez Canyon possesses spectacular red and buff canyon walls and is well known locally for its scenic qualities. The area was used heavily by the Utes and their predecessors. Some of the best examples of Indian rock art on the plateau can be found in Dominguez Canyon a few miles upstream from the Gunnison River. The Dominguez area was also the scene of the 1916 Delta County Sheep War. Howard Lathrop, a Montrose sheepman, herded his sheep across the Gunnison River onto "cattle country" and had his sheep shot for his efforts. A year later, Ben Lowe and

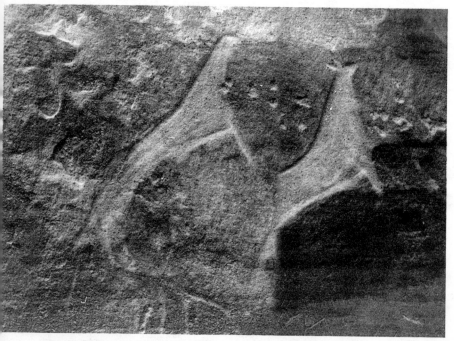

Ute horse petroglyph

deputy sheriff Cash Sampson traded fatal shots in Escalante Canyon. Many felt that Sampson was close to proving Ben's involvement in the sheep war when the shoot-out occurred.

Two long spurs that branch from the trail are worth exploring. The Long Mesa Trail and the Winter Camp Trail fork from the Dominguez Trail at mile 2.3 and mile 4, respectively. Both spurs head deep into the mesa country between the Dominguez and Escalante drainages.

A small population of desert bighorn sheep has been transplanted in the roadless section of Dominguez Creek.

2. BRUSHY RIDGE TRAIL

Elevation: 6,100–8,900 feet

Distance: 20 miles (one way)

Rating: Easy to strenuous

Season: June to September

Access: The lower terminus of the trail begins at Escalante Forks. The upper terminus branches from the Dominguez Trail 0.3 mile north of the Divide Road.

Maps: Trail Map One and U.S.G.S. Mesa County maps #5 & 6

Description: The general character of the trail is similar to the Dry Mesa and Love Mesa roads. The trail begins at Escalante Forks and follows the North Fork of Escalante Creek for 2.5 miles before it heads up a steep section that follows a small side canyon to the west rim of the North Fork. The trail then bears left through Bennetts and Spring basins. Once beyond Spring Basin, the trail climbs onto a broad bench just below Brushy Ridge. The predominant vegetation on the bench is scrub oak, but sagebrush, juniper, aspen and service-berry are well represented. This section of the trail offers numerous views of the Escalante Breaks far below. About five miles from the upper terminus the trail circumvents Snipe Mountain. The remainder of the trail contours in and out

Brushy Ridge Trail

of aspen groves and rolling meadows adjacent to the headwaters of Dominguez Creek.

Highlights: The land surrounding the Brushy Ridge Trail is full of reminders of days gone by. Near Bennetts Basin is an Indian wickiup village, which has been fenced to protect it from grazing cattle. Many other aboriginal sites are located in the vicinity. Several old buildings and cow camps can be found near the trail. One of the best preserved is Grampa's cabin in the Barclay Creek drainage.

The Brushy Ridge Trail, also known as the McCarty Trail, was used by the

McCarty Gang when they held up the Delta Farmers and Merchants Bank in 1893. The robbery turned out to be a nightmare for the gang. Tom McCarty was the only member of the gang to survive the heist. He fled to the La Sal Mountains in Utah, then moved to the Northwest after things had cooled off. The gang had stashed a sizeable amount of money in Tabeguache Canyon before the robbery, but never returned to reclaim it. Years later a relative of Tom's returned with a map, but attempts to relocate the stash were unsuccessful. It is commonly thought that the trail was named for the gang, but the trail was known as the McCarty Trail before the gang used it. The trail was used by Justin McCarty to graze his mules which were used in the Ouray mines.

3. LOVE MESA ROAD

Elevation:	6,100-9,600 feet
Distance:	22 miles (one way)
Rating:	Easy to moderate
Season:	The road opens around mid-June
Access:	The lower end of the road begins at Escalante Forks. The upper trailhead takes off from the Divide Road 2.5 miles northwest of Windy Point. The road can also be reached from the Sawmill Mesa and Delta-Nucla roads.
Maps:	Trail Map One, U.S.G.S. Mesa County map #6 and Montrose County map #3
Description:	The Love Mesa Road can best be described by dividing the road into equal parts. The lower half contours along the eastern slope of Escalante Creek for five miles before it begins a steady looping ascent to Love Mesa, which overlooks the confluence of the East and Middle forks of Escalante Creek. The lower half is remarkably smooth, but Escalante Creek poses a sizeable obstacle during spring runoff. The upper half starts at the Divide Road and quickly climbs to the crest of the plateau. Soon the road drops through a dense stand of spruce and fir. In a few miles, groves of aspens are encountered which, in turn, give way to an open forest of ponderosa pine. The upper half of the

Escalante Canyon from the Love Mesa Road

road is bumpy and rutted in places. It can be muddy after a heavy rain.

Highlights: Love Mesa was named after John Love, an early rancher in the area. The mesa sits between the East and Middle forks of Escalante Creek. Love Mesa is and has been the scene of logging operations. The large ponderosa pines make excellent lumber. During the recent pine beetle infestation, the trees acquired a steel-blue tint that was highly sought for interior decorating. The intimate forest scenery and the vistas from the mesa's north rim rank as some of the best on the plateau. Around the turn of the century, Love Mesa was still grizzly country. The grizzlies were hunted down as a threat to the cattle industry. Bear Pen Gulch near the south end of Love Mesa was the scene of one of many attempts to rid the plateau of the silvertips.

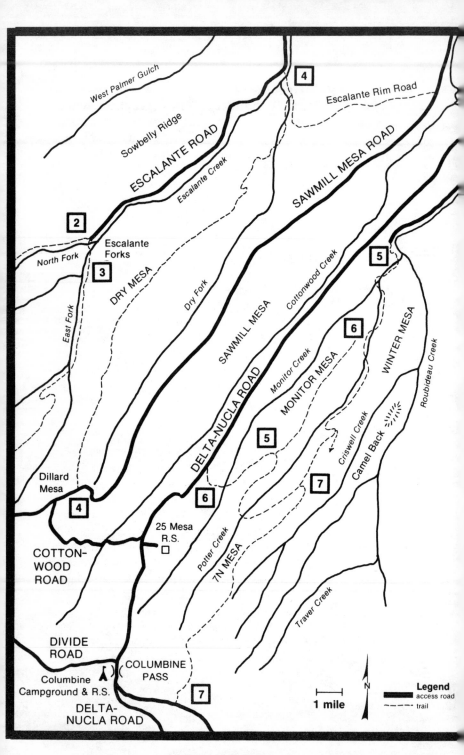

Trail Map Two

4. DRY MESA ROAD

Elevation:	5,000–8,000 feet
Distance:	20 miles (one way)
Rating:	Easy to strenuous
Season:	The lower six miles are open by April. The upper 14 miles are open by late May. The complete trail can be biked through the summer, but the lower section is hot. A prime time to ride the whole road is late August through September.
Access:	The Dry Mesa Road trailhead begins six miles up the Escalante Road from Highway 50. Access is also possible off Sawmill Mesa Road below Dillard Mesa. During the spring runoff, the Escalante Creek crossing is dangerous. Another access to the trail is by way of the Escalante Rim Road which branches from the Sawmill Mesa Road near the Roubideau Honor Camp. The Rim Road is marked on the U.S.G.S. Delta County map #2. The Rim Road drops off the east rim of the Dry Fork of Escalante Creek to connect with the Dry Mesa Road one mile from the Escalante Road trailhead.
Maps:	Trail Map Two, U.S.G.S. Delta County map #2, Montrose County map #1 and Mesa County map #6
Description:	The Dry Mesa Road initially travels up

the Dry Fork. The riding is easy, but bumpy, due to numerous stream crossings. At mile 3, the road suddenly begins a twisted, steep three-mile ascent to the rim of Dry Mesa. Once on Dry Mesa, the terrain smooths out for a long gentle climb to the road's upper terminus below Dillard Mesa.

Highlights: The road is an outstanding canyon/mesa trail. The canyon is 800 feet deep when the trail begins its climb out of the Dry Fork. The surrounding terrain is rugged and the scenery is spectacular. The interplay between the rusts and buffs of the rock walls and the green of

Dry Mesa Road switchbacks

the pinyon and juniper trees is dramatic.

In the early days, the Escalante drainages were a popular spot for mountain lion hunting. Today, cougars still roam the canyons of the plateau, but are protected from hunters. An ambitious 15-year project by the U.S. Fish and Wildlife Service, headed by Allan Anderson, studies the puma's habits and response to civilization. Scientific endeavors in the Escalante area are not limited to wildlife. Near the upper end of the Dry Mesa Road is a world-class dinosaur bone quarry. Brigham Young University staff have spent many years at the quarry uncovering some of the largest dinosaur bones in the world. Next to the road a short distance up the Dry Fork is a large historic and prehistoric rock art panel, with bear paws, men on horseback, and two finely executed horses incised in the rock.

5. POTTER CREEK ROAD

Elevation:	5,400–7,500 feet
Distance:	17 miles (one way)
Rating:	Overall the trail is moderate with two short steep sections
Season:	The lower eight miles open by mid-April. The upper section is passable by late May. Caution should be exercised when crossing Potter Creek during spring runoff. The prime time to bike the road is late August to September.
Access:	The road can be joined at two different points. The lower access road forks from the Delta-Nucla Road in Roubideau Canyon. Follow the road up Roubideau Canyon 5.5 miles to a small corral. The upper access is the Monitor Mesa Road (see the Monitor Mesa Road description). The Potter Creek Road branches from the Monitor Mesa Road at mile 4.
Maps:	Trail Map Two and U.S.G.S. Montrose County map #1
Description:	The Potter Creek Road has been described by many local jeepers as one of the roughest on the plateau. It is a canyon biker's paradise. The road initially follows Monitor Creek, then turns up Potter Creek. The first seven miles follow the canyon floor. The road is washed out in several places, and the

Potter Creek Road stream crossing

many stream crossings are rocky. The canyon averages 500 to 800 feet in depth and rises from the streambed in a series of steep slopes and cliffs. At mile 8 the road climbs out of the canyon west of the Saddle. By mile 9 the trail enters Potter Basin and continues on a long U-shaped course to Monitor Mesa.

Highlights: Potter Creek and Basin were named after one of several breeding stallions owned by the Roberts Brothers, who settled the area soon after the Utes were removed. Potter Creek is one of the major tributaries of Roubideau Creek. In late summer stretches of the creek dry up. The vegetation along the stream is dense—cottonwoods, willows, scrub oak, wild rose, virgin's bower and ponderosa pine are common. Watch out for poison ivy! Sagebrush, pinyon and juniper, mormon tea, and yucca grace the canyon slopes. Be sure to spend some time investigating the streambed. Mountain lion, raccoon, coyote, and deer tracks can be found at the water's edge. From the Saddle about halfway up the trail, the Camel Back rises up to the east. The Camel Back is the centerpiece for a BLM wilderness study area. This wild and rugged place is a prime example of the plateau's canyon/mesa country that has resisted man's imprint. One spur of the Potter Creek Road is a rough jeep trail that snakes deep into Criswell Basin. The Criswell Basin trail branches from the road as it passes west of the Saddle. The spur travels five-plus miles before it dead-ends. It is well worth the extra time and energy spent to get there.

6. MONITOR MESA ROAD

Elevation: 6,600–7,500 feet

Distance: 18 miles (round trip)

Rating: Moderate

Season: Mid-May to June, and again in the fall
                prior to hunting season

Access: The Monitor Mesa Road branches from
                the Delta-Nucla Road approximately
                14 miles from Roubideau Creek. The
                road is located near the National Forest
                boundary marked by a cattle guard.

Maps: Trail Map Two and U.S.G.S. Montrose
                County map #1

Description: The first few miles contour around the
                benches adjacent to Monitor Creek and
                the Lee reservoirs before climbing the
                western flank of Monitor Mesa. From
                the rim of the mesa, much of the Monitor
                Creek area can be seen. On the bench
                directly below, several meadows and
                buildings can be seen, part of the old Ed
                Lee place. The road forks just off the
                rim. The right fork is the Forty-One
                Trail which eventually reaches the
                Divide Road near Columbine Pass. The
                left fork leads to Monitor Mesa. In a
                mile or so the road again forks. The
                right fork is the upper terminus of the
                Potter Creek Road. The left fork con-
                tinues down Monitor Mesa to its north-
                ern end. The overlook at the end of the

road offers an outstanding view of the Monitor-Potter Creek confluence.

Highlights: The first few miles wind through stands of ponderosa pine, scrub oak, serviceberry, sagebrush, pinyon and juniper. In the spring, wildflowers abound. Once on Monitor Mesa, the rider will no doubt notice a lack of trees. Back in the 1960s, the BLM chained the mesa top as part of a range improvement project. The rider may also notice a profusion of chipped stone on the mesa. These artifacts are remnants of a culture that inhabited western Colorado for several thousand years. The area has numerous archaeological sites, several of which were excavated in the early 1960s as part of the Ute Prehistory Project.

The vistas from Monitor Mesa are excellent. Distant views of the Grand Mesa, the West Elk Mountains, the Black Canyon of the Gunnison and the Uncompahgre Valley are possible.

7. 7N MESA ROAD

Elevation: 7,200–9,200 feet

Distance: 11 miles (one way)

Rating: Easy

Season: The lower end of the road usually opens up by mid-May. The upper end is passable around mid-June.

Access: The lower trailhead merges with the Potter Creek Road six miles from Monitor Mesa. The upper trailhead branches from the Divide Road 4.4 miles east of Columbine Pass.

Maps: Trail Map Two and U.S.G.S. Montrose County map #1

Description: From the upper trailhead the road is an easy, smooth ride for several miles. Once past the gate near the Beach Cow Camp, the road deteriorates to a jeep road. About a mile beyond the gate, the terrain steepens for a short distance before flattening out again on 7N Mesa.

Highlights: The handle "7N" is derived from the name of an early cattle company. The 7N Mesa Road parallels a ramp that runs perpendicular to the plateau's crest. The change in elevation is hardly noticeable. Along this road are excellent views showing the interplay between the different vegetation zones. Starting from the Divide Road and working down in elevation, spruce and fir will be found growing in dense forests adjacent to the Divide Road. As the traveler begins to coast downhill, a few aspens can be seen intermingled with the spruce and fir. Gradually, thick stands of aspen dominate the scenery, with an occasional Douglas fir. As the rider drops in elevation, ponderosa pine show up with increasing frequency until they replace the aspen. At this point, the traveler has reached the gate near the Beach Cow Camp. Beyond the gate a rich mingling of trees and shrubs surrounds the nearby meadow. It is no wonder wildlife abound in this zone. The scrub oak are especially large in this area. Once past the meadow, the road steepens a bit through a mixed stand of scrub oak and serviceberry. Soon they give way to the pinyon-juniper woodland and sage flats as the road merges with Potter Basin Road.

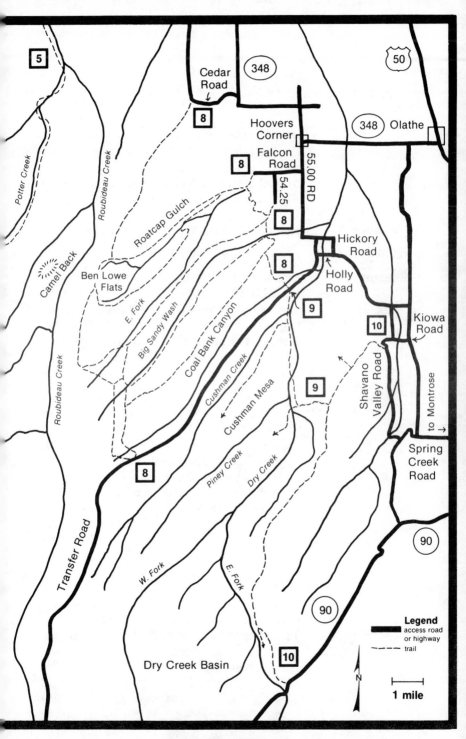

Trail Map Three

8. EAST ROUBIDEAU RIM TRAILS

Elevation: 5,500–7,600 feet

Distance: 50+ miles (one way)

Rating: Easy to moderate

Season: The lower elevations in this area are rideable from late March through May, and again in the fall. The roads at higher altitudes open up in early May. The heat of the summer makes this area undesirable during June, July and August.

Access: At least five access points provide a variety of biking opportunities. Access to the upper reaches of this locale can be gained nine miles up the Transfer Road. Forest Service roads 509 and 542 begin near the Forest Service boundary. The other four access points start in or near the valley floor. The first is located directly opposite the Dry Creek Road trailhead on the Transfer Road. It parallels the powerline. The West Transfer Road can be reached by driving south from Hoovers Corner to Falcon Road, then driving west to 54.25 Road and again turning south. The Roatcap Gulch Trail begins at the end of Falcon Road. Pass through three gates, then bear right around a flood control dam. The last access point is located north and west of Hoovers Corner. Follow Colorado Highway 348 3.25 miles to Cedar

Roubideau Trail

Road. Drive 1.5 miles west on Cedar Road until a BLM access road is encountered.

Maps:	Trail Map Three and U.S.G.S. Montrose County map #1
Description:	The numerous roads in this area parallel several of many small mesas that fan out from the east rim of Roubideau Canyon. The intervening drainages are shallow, and flow intermittently. The terrain is easy to moderate, but short hill climbs will be encountered along the powerline road and in Roatcap Gulch. Biking surface ranges from sandy to rocky.
Highlights:	The interconnecting nature of the roads permits the rider to organize a number of loop trips, bypassing the need to shuttle vehicles or retrace routes. One particularly nice loop takes off along the jeep road that runs west of Roatcap Gulch. It winds its way to Ben Lowe Flats, then returns via Roatcap Gulch.

Ben Lowe Flats was named after a colorful man who lived in western Colorado during the early 1900s. He liked to ride spirited horses and was a crack shot with firearms. Remains of one of Lowe's cabins can be found in Roubideau Canyon. Three foot trails drop off the east rim of Roubideau Canyon in the vicinity of Ben Lowe Flats.

In a canyon west of Roatcap Gulch, Dr. Marie Wormington, a noted anthropologist, excavated the Moore rockshelter in the 1930s. From her investigations, she was able to document a culture that inhabited western Colorado for thousands of years. The people hunted and gathered resources to sustain themselves. Dr. Wormington named this Archaic culture the Uncompahgre Complex, a variant of the Desert Culture found throughout the Great Basin. One of the best preserved examples of prehistoric rock art can be found in Roatcap Gulch.

Deer as well as coyote, rabbits, packrats, golden eagles, canyon wrens and loggerhead shrikes populate the many canyons in the area.

9. DRY CREEK ROAD

Elevation: 6,000–6,400 feet

Distance: 5 miles (one way)

Rating: Easy to moderate

Season: Year-round when road is dry. The road
               is quite slippery when wet, and the
               crossing of Dry Creek during spring
               runoff and heavy summer rains can be
               dangerous.

Access: The road branches from the Transfer
               Road two miles from Holly Road, near
               one of the towers that supports the
               powerline. Access is also possible from
               the Dry Creek Rim Road 4.5 miles up
               from the Shavano Valley Road.

Maps: Trail Map Three and U.S.G.S. Montrose
               County map #1

Description: From either trailhead the road wastes
               no time dropping to the floor of Dry
               Creek. The Transfer Road access begins
               with a 250-foot descent in 0.25 mile, and
               the Dry Creek Rim Road access drops
               400 feet in one mile. The road has only
               one stream crossing about midway be-
               tween the trailheads, but it can be tricky
               during high water. Much of the road is
               on clay that is slippery when wet.

Highlights: Dry Creek is one of the major drainages
               on the north side of the plateau. It is
               lined with cottonwood, scrub oak and

tamarisk, providing excellent habitat for small birds, deer, raptors, beaver and waterfowl.

Early in the twentieth century, the lower end of the canyon was the home of a large ranching operation. The spread was nicknamed "Owlhoot." During the days of Prohibition, the ranch hosted Saturday night dances complete with a band and moonshine. Very little of the ranch remains today, the victim of a BLM land swap.

Dry Creek was also the scene of significant prehistoric activity. Several archaeological sites can be found on the canyon floor and along the canyon's rims. In the early 1960s the Chipeta Chapter of the Colorado Archaeological Society and the Ute Prehistory Project excavated a number of sites along Dry Creek. A short distance up Cushman Creek, a tributary of Dry Creek, is a large boulder covered with Indian petroglyphs. There is also an "Indian Flint Mine" tucked away along the east wall of the canyon. The stone quarried at the mine is chert, a common tool material. The first settlers found the mine covered with soot and ash. The Indians no doubt heated the rock to splinter off workable chunks.

Two spurs break away from the Dry Creek Road, adding distance and scenic variety to the pedaling possibilities. The Cushman Mesa Road branches off the Dry Creek Road approximately one mile from the Transfer Road trailhead. The route immediately climbs up the northern flank of Cushman Mesa, then moderates for several miles before

Dry Creek Road descent

ending at private property. On the other end of the Dry Creek Road, the Piney Creek Trail splits about one mile from the Rim Road. It ascends a low bench on the west side of Dry Creek and turns southwest along Piney Creek, eventually topping out on Cushman Mesa.

10. DRY CREEK RIM ROAD

Elevation: 5,800–7,900 feet

Distance: 14 miles (one way)

Rating: Easy

Season: The lower section opens up by late March. The upper section is usually dry by early May. The entire road remains open through the summer until fall.

Access: The road roughly parallels the east rim of Dry Creek. The lower terminus is located near the north end of the Shavano Valley Road. Access from Montrose is by way of Spring Creek, 58.75 and Kiowa roads. The upper terminus is located several miles up Highway 90 just before it descends to cross the East Fork of Dry Creek.

Maps: Trail Map Three and U.S.G.S. Montrose County Map #1

Description: The general character of the road is of a gradual climb, interrupted by a few short hill climbs. The road begins in low grasslands adjacent to the valley floor, then passes through sagebrush flats and the pinyon-juniper stands, before reaching pure stands of scrub oak. Several spurs from the Rim Road are worth noting. One follows the powerline and leaves the Rim Road two miles from its lower terminus. Another spur forks from the Rim Road 3.5 miles below

Dry Creek Rim Road spur

the upper terminus. It drops into Dry Creek for two miles before a locked gate is encountered.

Highlights: The diversity of vegetation along the road is impressive. In the fall, sweet nuts can be gathered from the cones of the pinyon trees. The pinyon nut crop and the large numbers of wild game attracted prehistoric people to the area. The Rim Road crosses the tableland that divides Shavano Valley and Dry Creek, and contains a high density of archaeological sites. Many of the sites have been excavated by professional archaeologists. The most scenic spot along the road is Windy Gap, a natural break in the mesa between Shavano Valley and Dry Creek. Longtime residents of Montrose originally referred to the road as the pipeline road, because it followed the pipeline that provided the town of Olathe with its domestic water.

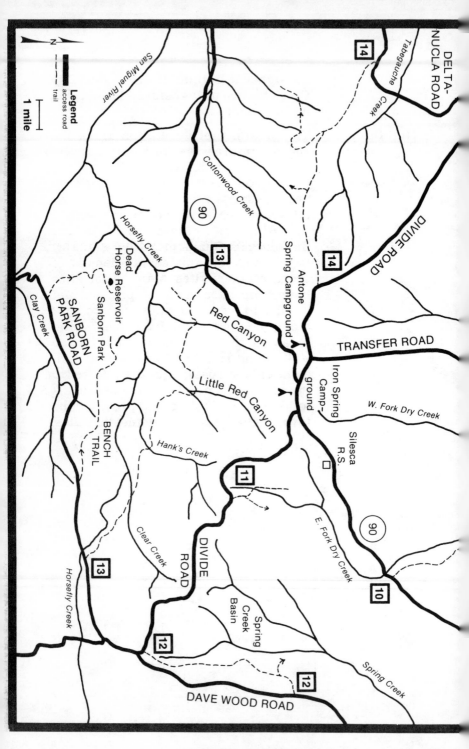

Trail Map Four

11. BEAVER DAMS ROAD

Elevation:	9,200-9,700 feet
Distance:	4+ miles (round trip)
Rating:	Easy
Season:	Mid-June to September
Access:	The Beaver Dams Road (signed Road 524) branches from the Divide Road at mile 73.5. (See Divide Road Log in Chapter Six.) The Beaver Dams Road is 5.8 miles from the Divide Road/Highway 90 intersection and 9.2 miles from the Divide Road/Dave Wood intersection.
Maps:	Trail Map Four, U.S.G.S. Montrose County map #4 and Ouray County map #1
Description:	The Beaver Dams Road bears north from the Divide Road. It gradually descends along the slopes of Beaver Dams Creek, a tributary of Dry Creek. At mile 0.6 the road intersects with the Dry Creek Pack Trail to the left—the trailhead is mismarked "Dry Fork Trail." The pack trail can be biked a short distance before deadfall timber impedes progress. Directly opposite the Dry Creek Pack Trail trailhead is a jeep trail which winds through a dense aspen forest. It provides several more miles of bikeable road.
Highlights:	The Beaver Dams Road is one of many

short roads that branch from the Divide Road, some of which provided access to logging operations. Along the road, meadows created by clearcut logging are filled with wildflowers and young trees. Many large aspen trees grow beside the road. Some good examples of aspen tree art are found along the Dry Creek Pack Trail 100 yards from the Beaver Dams Road. Aspen tree art can be found throughout the plateau. The best was created between the 1930s and the 1950s by sheepherders who spent the summer months tending their flocks. Due to the short life span of aspens and the recent increase of logging, much of the tree art is gone. The Forest Service recognizes the uniqueness of the tree art and is recording it before the aspens are harvested.

Near Beaver Dams Road

12. SPRING CREEK RIM TRAIL

Elevation:	8,000-9,200 feet
Distance:	6 miles (one way)
Rating:	Easy
Season:	The trail usually dries out by early June and remains open through September.
Access:	Drive up Dave Wood Road nine miles to the cattleguard which marks the Forest Service boundary. This trail is a jeep road that begins just inside the boundary and heads due west. The upper end of the trail merges with the Divide Road 0.3 mile north of the Divide Road-Dave Wood Road intersection.
Maps:	Trail Map Four, U.S.G.S. Montrose County map #4 and Ouray County map #1
Description:	The trail parallels the east rim of the East Fork of Spring Creek. It initially passes through a reforestation project, but soon winds through open stands of ponderosa pine and scrub oak. Aspen and fir, which provide shady relief on a hot summer day, are found roadside higher up on the trail.
Highlights:	Views of wild and pristine Spring Creek Basin are possible from several vantage points along the trail. The eastern trailhead of the Spring Creek Trail branches from the Rim Trail one mile from its lower terminus. The Spring Creek Trail

is bikeable for one-half mile before it narrows to a foot trail and descends into the basin. The basin holds the three upper forks of Spring Creek.

The display of fall colors along the Rim Trail is superb. The gold hues of the aspen contrast nicely with the reds and oranges of the scrub oak. In the spring, before there are leaves on the trees, pasqueflower, spring beauty and fawn lily cover the forest floor.

Spring Creek Rim Road

13. HANKS VALLEY ROAD

Elevation:	7,600–8,300 feet
Distance:	12 miles (one way)
Rating:	Moderate
Season:	June to September
Access:	Hanks Valley begins three miles west of the Dave Wood-Sanborn Park Road intersection. Another access point is possible from south Highway 90 12 miles east of the San Miguel River. This access is rough and steep in places as it drops into Red Canyon.
Maps:	Trail Map Four and U.S.G.S. Montrose County map #4
Description:	The Hanks Valley Road contours along the north bench of Horsefly Creek and crosses four of its tributaries. The road eventually rolls out to the point between Red and Little Red canyons. The trail is rocky in places and can be rutted and muddy during rainy periods.
Highlights:	This road offers the biker a little of everything: stream crossings, hill climbs, flat stretches and downhill runs. The countryside also offers a variety of scenery. The aspen groves overlooking the road are prime sheep grazing country. Much of the tree art on the plateau graces aspens in this area. One particular aspen has unusual carvings that

Hanks Valley Road map check

resemble some of the local Indian rock art. The Hanks Valley area is prime deer and elk habitat. Bull elk can be heard bugling at daybreak during the September rut. Far below the road is Horsefly Creek whose headwaters begin on the slopes of Horsefly Peak. Local lore credits a sheepherder with naming the peak because it resembles a fly from the right vantage point. On the south side of the creek is a large bench which contains Sanborn Park. Two bikeable trails, Bench Trail and Deadhorse Reservoir Road, are located on the bench.

14. HAUSER ROAD

Elevation:	8,100–9,800 feet
Distance:	12 miles (one way)
Rating:	Easy to moderate
Season:	Mid-June through September
Access:	Access to the Hauser Road is possible from two major access roads. The road intersects the Delta-Nucla Road 12 miles from Nucla, and the Divide Road three miles west of the Antone Spring Campground.
Maps:	Trail Map Four and U.S.G.S. Montrose County maps #1 & 4
Description:	The upper section of the trail weaves through stands of spruce and fir, then switchbacks among groves of aspens. The road eventually levels off and follows the southern ridge of upper Tabeguache Creek. The lower half of the trail contours through mixed stands of oakbrush, juniper, ponderosa pine and aspens. The road is dusty when dry and can be slippery when wet. Several spurs take off from the Hauser Road, traveling down into the drainages south of the road. One spur branches from the main trail approximately seven miles from the Divide Road. The spur passes by a fuelwood gathering area as it drops into the North Fork of Cottonwood Creek. The other spur drops into the Little

Hauser Road spur

Cottonwood Creek vicinity. The Little Cottonwood spur leaves the main trail 3.5 miles from the Divide Road. Both spurs amble into some wonderfully rugged terrain.

Highlights:
Wildflowers such as yellow lupine, larkspur and columbine can be seen along the road. Deer frequent the meadows. Excellent views of the San Miguel River valley, the Wilson Peaks, the Dolores Peaks and Lone Cone are possible. The La Sal and Abajo mountains in Utah can be seen on a clear day. Near the half-way point on the road is an exceptional view of upper Tabeguache

Creek. Across the road from the view-point is a large, gnarled scrub oak.

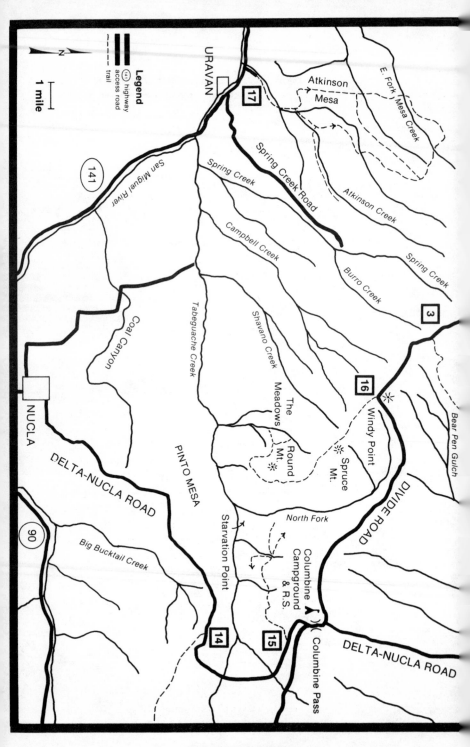

Trail Map Five

15. COPPER KING ROAD

Elevation:	7,600–8,800 feet
Distance:	13+ miles (round trip)
Rating:	Moderate
Season:	Mid-June to September
Access:	Copper King Road branches from the Delta–Nucla Road 1.6 miles south of Columbine Pass.
Maps:	Trail Map Five and U.S.G.S. Montrose County map #1
Description:	The Copper King Road gradually drops into Tabeguache Basin east of Tabeguache Creek's North Fork. It eventually deteriorates to a faint pack trail that traverses the North Fork. The road is smooth, winding through small meadows and large stands of ponderosa pine. Additional biking can be done on two spurs. The first spur forks from the main road at mile 5.0 and continues for 1.5 miles. The second spur, the Grassy Lake Trail, branches from the road at mile 5.3, across from the Copper King Mine. The Grassy Lake Trail heads deep into Tabeguache Basin. Approximate distance to Grassy Lake is 5.5 miles.
Highlights:	The Copper King Road has outstanding scenic qualities. Views of the thousand-foot-deep Tabeguache Canyon are awe-

inspiring. Tabeguache Basin supports a sizeable population of elk and deer plus a substantial number of bobcat, beaver, bear and cougar. The Ute Indians found the Tabeguache area quite hospitable. The English translation for Tabeguache is "place where the snow melts first." A short distance beyond the Copper King Mine, the road crosses an old Indian trail that comes out of Tabeguache Canyon. If this trail into Tabeguache Canyon can be found, it leads to a large rockshelter a couple of miles downstream. The rockshelter, named Tabeguache Cave I, was excavated by the late C. T. Hurst, a Western State College professor and founder of the Colorado Archaeological Society. Hurst's findings changed the archaeological thinking of his day. Buried beneath the surface of the cave was a wealth of artifacts and features that had all the markings of the Basketmaker culture of the Four Corners area. Hurst found evidence of the Basketmakers, as well as the Pueblo culture, in several tributaries of the San Miguel River.

A prominent feature in Tabeguache Basin is Starvation Point. Long-time residents relate stories of daring rescues of trapped cattle from the bench. Once cattle dropped onto the bench, they wouldn't leave, and as winter set in they became trapped and would starve. A customary practice in recent years involved flying over Starvation Point in search of stranded cattle. If enough cattle were spotted, four or five men on horseback broke a trail through the snow, rounded up the cattle and drove them out.

Tabeguache Basin from the Divide Road

16. FORTY-SEVEN TRAIL

Elevation: 7,500–9,600 feet

Distance: 16 miles (round trip)

Rating: Moderately strenuous

Season: Late June to September

Access: The trail is a jeep road which branches from the Divide Road at Windy Point.

Maps: Trail Map Five and U.S.G.S. Montrose County maps #3 & 4

Description: The trail initially bears southeast and weaves through stands of aspen for 2.5 miles. It then drops onto a bench directly below Spruce Mountain, but soon leaves the bench. Two gates are encountered before the trail makes a steady descent to the west side of the North Fork of Tabeguache Creek. At mile 5 the road turns south and descends to a series of benches east of Round Mountain. Fallen trees and boggy areas will no doubt be encountered along the way. The trail then contours around the southern and western flanks of Round Mountain. Near the end of the trail it branches. Either branch continues for a short distance before private land blocks further progress. The Forest Service travel map shows a possible access by way of The Meadows, but there is no public right-of-way through The Meadows.

Highlights: The Forty-Seven Trail was named after the 47 Cattle Company. The outfit took its name from the shape of the snowbank on the mountain north of Nucla that resembles the numbers 4 and 7. The original Forty-Seven Trail climbed the palisades above The Meadows, crossed the present jeep road near the 47 cow camp, then continued up and over the crest of the plateau.

Herbert Loucks, a long-time resident of western Colorado, tells a story that captures the flavor of the early days. Herb had taken a day off to prospect for uranium. He dropped off the benches along the Forty-Seven Trail and headed for Tabeguache Creek. As he descended, small rocks pelted him from above. The regularity of the pelting puzzled him until he retraced his steps. Much to his surprise, fresh cougar tracks overlaid his original footprints.

Evidence of prehistoric activity in the vicinity of the Forty-Seven Trail abounds. On a bench northeast of Round Mountain, an old Ute racetrack and rockshelter can be found. There is also an Indian trail that climbs out of the North Fork and passes along the benches east of Round Mountain before it descends into Tabeguache Creek near the mouth of Forty-Seven Creek.

Local lore places the buried cache of the McCarty gang somewhere in the canyons near the Forty-Seven Trail.

17. ATKINSON CREEK ROAD

Elevation:	5,100–6,300 feet
Distance:	11 miles (round trip)
Rating:	Easy
Season:	April, May and again in September
Access:	The Atkinson Creek Road branches from Highway 141 two miles down canyon from the main Uravan turnoff. The road is marked RD T17. A short distance up the road, a pair of roads merge from the left. The first is marked "Do Not Enter." It is the outlet of a one-way road that drops into the canyon from the uranium mines on Atkinson Mesa. The second is the entrance to the mines road.
Maps:	Trail Map Five and U.S.G.S. Montrose County map #3
Description:	The Atkinson Creek Road follows the canyon floor. The road crosses the creek several times, but it is easily negotiated, even during spring runoff. At mile 2.2 and 3.3, the road forks. At both intersections, bear right. Be sure to close the gates that are encountered. The last mile of the road is a rutted, narrow two-track.
Highlights:	The Atkinson Road is an excellent early-season warmup route. Distance and difficulty can be added to the route by taking one of the two roads that fork

from the main road at mile 2.2 and 3.3. Both roads climb up to Atkinson Mesa and proceed in a northerly direction. Atkinson Mesa has a maze of roads, so be sure to map out a route carefully.

The south rim of Atkinson Mesa offers an excellent view of the confluence of the San Miguel and Dolores rivers. In the 1880s, gold was panned from Mesa Creek Flats below the confluence. In 1889, an ambitious two-year project was undertaken by the Montrose Placer Mining Company. The firm bought up the mining claims along the Dolores River near Mesa Creek Flats and built

Atkinson Creek Road

an eight-mile flume along the northern wall of San Miguel and Dolores canyons. The flume provided enough hydraulic pressure to allow placer mining. The wooden flume, six feet wide and four feet deep, was supported by brackets imbedded into the canyon's sandstone walls. The hanging flume was a huge success from an engineering standpoint, but the gold was so fine that it couldn't be retrieved from the sluice boxes. The operation was a complete loss. Today, segments of the hanging flume can be seen from Highway 141.

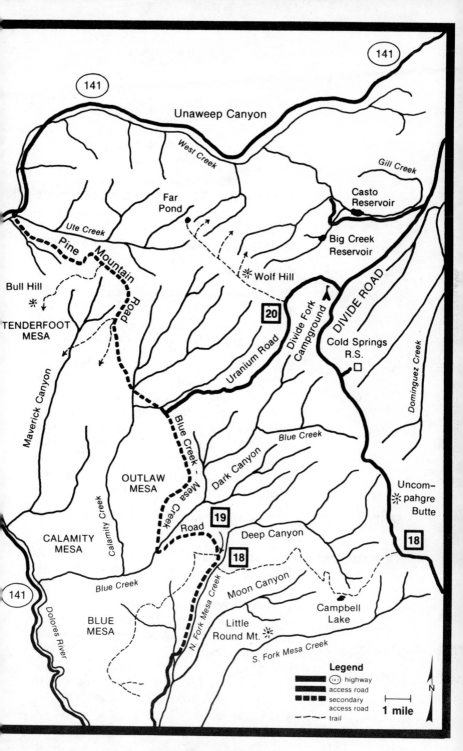

Trail Map Six

18. CAMPBELL POINT ROAD

Elevation:	6,000–9,200 feet
Distance:	10 miles (one way)
Rating:	Strenuous
Season:	The lower section dries out by mid-April while the upper segment is passable by mid-June. The entire road remains open through September.
Access:	The Campbell Point Road is reached by driving up the Mesa Creek–Blue Creek Road. Eleven miles from Highway 141, the Campbell Point Road forks to the right just as the access road begins to climb out of Mesa Creek. There is usually a sign marking the road. The road merges with the Divide Road two miles south of Uncompahgre Butte.
Maps:	Trail Map Six and U.S.G.S. Mesa County map #5
Description:	The road initially crosses the North Fork of Mesa Creek, then steadily contours its way across the slope below the plateau's western escarpment. The road gains 2,000 feet in four miles. As the escarpment is reached, the road switchbacks several times before topping out on the rim of Campbell Point. The road flattens out for the remainder of its course. If this road is attempted during the summer months, be sure to get an early start to avoid the heat of the day.

Campbell Lake, Campbell Point Road

Highlights: Campbell Point was named after a local resident who murdered his business partner and tossed his body over a nearby cliff. The partner's body was found, Campbell was convicted of murder and imprisoned.

The terrain along this trail is rugged and varied. The uplifting of the plateau has tilted and twisted the land along the lower section of the road. The upper segment winds along a wide ridge that separates the North and South forks of Mesa Creek. The road passes through the pinyon-juniper, oak-ponderosa pine, and aspen-fir vegetation belts. The

119

scenery is outstanding with excellent views of the La Sal Mountains. Many side roads will be encountered, so keep the map handy. A small lake is located at the road's halfway point. Good campsites can be found at the beginning of the trail soon after it crosses the North Fork of Mesa Creek, and near the Divide Road.

19. BLUE MESA ROAD

Elevation: 5,900-6,200 feet

Distance: 18 miles (round trip)

Rating: Easy, with a few short hill climbs

Season: Late April to May and again in September

Access: The Blue Mesa Road branches to the left from the Mesa Creek-Blue Creek Road at mile 12, one mile beyond the Campbell Point Road turnoff.

Maps: Trail Map Six, U.S.G.S. Montrose County map #3 and Mesa County map #5

Description: The road starts by contouring in and out of shallow drainage, then turns south along a ridge. At mile 2 the road reaches Blue Mesa. At mile 4 the road jogs west, then again heads south over the mesa's broad plain. At mile 9 the road ends near the south rim of the mesa. There are several side roads that wander from the main road that are worth exploring.

Highlights: The terrain surrounding Blue Mesa could easily be mistaken for the canyon country in Utah. The geologic formations that are exposed along the Dolores River and the nearby canyons are also found in Canyonlands and Arches national parks. Blue Mesa is covered with sage, pinyon pine and juniper. Wildflowers and wildlife abound on the mesa.

La Sal Mountains in Utah, from the Blue Mesa Trail

Blue Mesa received its name from the copper blue color of the Morrison formation that forms the slopes of the mesa. The panoramic view from Blue Mesa is superb, offering excellent vistas of the Dolores River, Sewemup Mesa, the La Sal Mountains, the plateau's crest and the nearby canyons of Mesa and Blue creeks.

Blue Mesa is in the heart of uranium country. Prospects and mines dot the landscape. The carnotite ore from the mines was hauled to mills by way of the Uranium and Pine Mountain roads. The Pine Mountain Road, which connects Uranium Road with Unaweep Canyon, offers access to biking opportunities on Flat Top, Calamity and Tenderfoot mesas.

20. RIM TRAIL

Elevation:	9,000–9,300 feet
Distance:	11 miles (round trip)
Rating:	Easy
Season:	Mid-June to September
Access:	The Rim Trail branches from the Uranium Road 2.8 miles from Divide Fork.
Maps:	Trail Map Six and U.S.G.S. Mesa County map #5
Description:	The Rim Trail parallels the rim of the plateau's southwest escarpment. It is sandy, rocky and rutted, but the rough areas are easily circumvented. The trail gradually climbs through open meadows and aspen groves. At mile 3 the trail passes by Big Pond, the first of several natural ponds found along the Rim Trail. At mile 4.5 and 5.5, Rim Pond and Far Pond are encountered.
Highlights:	The ponds along the trail are small but picturesque. They are surrounded by water-loving plants and are dependable watering holes for a variety of wildlife. If the ponds are approached quietly, deer or waterfowl may be seen.

Once Big Pond is reached, the trail closely follows the rim of the escarpment. A short walk to the rim rewards the biker with a grand view of the terrain to the southwest. Directly below are Ute, Calamity, Cow and Indian creeks. Calamity, Tenderfoot and Flat Top mesas overlook the Dolores River Canyon. Beyond the canyon, Paradox Valley and the La Sal Mountains can be seen. The ruggedness of the plateau's canyon country can be fully appreciated.

Three trails intersect the Rim Trail. The Cabin, Little Creek and Basin trails, marked with a single 4x4 pole, are worth exploring.

SELECTED BIBLIOGRAPHY

GEOLOGY

Baars, Donald. **The Colorado Plateau, A Geologic History.** University of New Mexico Press. 1983.

Barnes, F. A. **Canyon Country Geology for the Layman and Rockhound.** Wasatch Publishers, Inc. 1978.

Chronic, John and Halka. **Prairie, Peak and Plateau.** Colorado Geological Survey. 1972.

Young, Robert and Joann. **Colorado West: Land of Geology and Wildflowers.** Wheelwright Press, Ltd. 1977.

NATURAL HISTORY

Elmore, Francis. **Shrubs and Trees of the Southwest Uplands.** Southwest Parks and Monuments Association. 1976.

Minor, Will. **Footprints in the Trail.** Historical Museum and Institute of Western Colorado. 1950.

Olin, George. **Mammals of the Southwest Mountains and Mesas.** Southwest Parks and Monuments Association. 1961.

Spellenberg, Richard. **The Audubon Society Field Guide to North American Wildflowers, Western Region.** Alfred A. Knopf, Inc. 1979.

Udvardy, Miklos. **The Audubon Society Field Guide to North American Birds, Western Region.** Alfred A. Knopf, Inc. 1977.

Young and Young. **Ibid.**

Zwinger, Ann. **Beyond the Aspen Grove.** Harper Colophon Books. 1970.

PREHISTORY

Barnes, F. A. **Canyon Country Prehistoric Rock Art.** Wasatch Publishers. 1982.

Buckles, William. "The Uncompahgre Complex: Historic Ute Archaeology and Prehistoric Archaeology of the Uncompahgre Plateau in West-Central Colorado." Ph.D. Dissertation (unpublished), University of Colorado, Boulder. 1964.

Cassells, E. Steve. **The Archaeology of Colorado.** Johnson Books. 1983.

McKern, W. C. **Western Colorado Petroglyphs.** Bureau of Land Management Cultural Resources Series No. 8. 1978.

Reed, Alan. **West Central Colorado Prehistoric Context Regional Research Design.** Denver: The State Historical Society of Colorado. 1984.

Wormington, H. Marie and Robert Lister. **Archaeological Investigations on the Uncompahgre Plateau in West Central Colorado.** Denver: Museum of Natural History. 1956.

HISTORY

Casebier, Caleb. **Twenty Sleeps West.** Thomas Printing. 1979.

Casebier, Caleb. **Yucca Seed.** Uncompahgre Publishing Co. 1980.

Emmitt, Robert. **The Last War Trail.** University of Oklahoma Press. 1954.

Lavender, David. **One Man's West.** Doubleday. 1956.

Look, Al. **1,000 Million Years on the Colorado Plateau.** Bell Publications. 1955.

Marshall, Muriel. **Uncompahgre.** Caxton Printers, Ltd. 1981.

Marshall, Muriel. **Red Hole in Time.** Texas A & M Press. 1988.

Musser, Eda Baker. **Trails and Trails.** 1986.

O'Rourke, Paul. **Frontier in Transition—A History of Southwestern Colorado.** Bureau of Land Management Cultural Resource Series No. 10. 1980.

Rockwell, Wilson. **Uncompahgre Country.** Sage Books. 1965.

Smith, P. David. **Ouray, Chief of the Utes.** Wayfinder Press. 1986.

MISCELLANEOUS

Brown, Tom. **Tom Brown's Field Guide to Wilderness Survival.** Berkeley Books. 1983.

Coello, Dennis. **The Mountain Bike Manual.** Dream Garden Press. 1985.

Fear, Gene. **Surviving the Unexpected Wilderness Emergency.** Survival Education Association. 1972.

Perry, John and Jane. **The Sierra Club Guide to the Natural Areas of Colorado and Utah.** Sierra Club Books. 1985.